# The Walt Disney World That Never Was

## Stories Behind the Amazing Imagineering Dreams That Never Came True

Christopher E. Smith

Theme Park Press
www.ThemeParkPress.com

Editor: Bob McLain
Layout: Artisanal Text

ISBN 978-1-68390-028-3
Printed in the United States of America

**Theme Park Press | www.ThemeParkPress.com**
Address queries to bob@themeparkpress.com

# Contents

# Introduction

*If the spark of an idea is strong, it will never fade away. Even if it travels only far enough to appear on that first piece of paper, there it will patiently remain until the time is right for it to re-ignite.*

— The Imagineers, *Walt Disney Imagineering: A Behind the Dreams Look at Making the Magic Real* (1996)

Pirates of the Caribbean, Big Thunder Mountain Railroad, and Splash Mountain are three of the most popular attractions in all of Walt Disney World. Each of these classic Disney experiences is synonymous with the Most Magical Place on Earth, and it is hard to imagine a Magic Kingdom without one of them, much less all three.

But what if I told you that on the Magic Kingdom's opening day, October 1, 1971, none of these fan favorites were even on the drawing board? Instead, the creative minds at Disney developed plans for a monumental concept known as Thunder Mesa that would have literally towered over Frontierland and forever changed the landscape of the world's most popular theme park. Set within the massive walls of an enormous Monument Valley mountain range, Thunder Mesa would have included perhaps the most popular attraction in all of Walt Disney World: an Old West version of Pirates of the Caribbean, with cowboys and bandits entertaining guests in lieu of rowdy buccaneers.

Have you (or more likely your children) been swept into an icy frenzy following the release of the 2013 Disney animated feature film *Frozen* and the introduction of such beloved characters as Anna, Elsa, Olaf, Sven, and Kristoff? What if I told you that four decades prior to the release of that film, one of Disney's most brilliant minds worked tirelessly to develop plans for a beautiful Enchanted Snow Palace that would have been located in the heart of Fantasyland and based upon the same Hans Christian Andersen fairy tale that inspired *Frozen*?

Do you enjoy strolling around Epcot's World Showcase Lagoon and experiencing the dining, shopping, shows, and cultural experiences that are beautifully displayed in each of the eleven World Showcase pavilions? What if I told you that in 1990, the Disney company announced plans for a new Soviet Union Pavilion that would have included a version of Moscow's Red Square and an enormous replica of Saint Basil's Cathedral, complete with ornate onion domes, serving as the pavilion's dramatic centerpiece?

Thunder Mesa, the Enchanted Snow Palace, and the Soviet Union Pavilion are just three examples at the tip of a creative iceberg of fascinating ideas and plans that never made it off of the drawing boards and into the Walt Disney World parks.

For more than five decades, Disney's most trusted Imagineers (the artists, architects, animators, engineers, designers, mechanics, and musicians that create the magic found throughout the parks) have invested thousands of hours thinking, sketching, designing, and testing attractions, shows, hotels, restaurants, and shops for the Walt Disney World Resort. Today, guests from around the world have the privilege of enjoying many of these concepts as they were actually constructed and placed into operation. However, unbeknownst to most Walt Disney World guests, there is also a long list of attractions, hotels, restaurants, and entire theme park lands that Disney's most creative minds poured their hearts and souls into developing but which never came to be.

But if an idea never actually made it into the parks, it must not have been that good in the first place—right? Nothing could be further from the truth. If completed, many of these concepts would have been jaw dropping, groundbreaking, and, dare I say it, better than many of the headliner experiences present in Walt Disney World today. However, due to a number of factors including excessive cost, politics, lack of technological capabilities, and old-fashioned bad timing, these ideas never saw the light of day. While some concepts never made it past the so-called "Blue Sky" phase of initial brainstorming and conceptualization, others were literally on the doorstep of being constructed.

Although it would be almost impossible to discuss every theme park concept dreamed up by Disney Imagineers that never made it into the parks, what follows is a collection of stories about the most significant, compelling, and downright fun ideas that you won't find in Walt Disney World today. In these stories, I will share the history and details of these wonderful ideas, why they were never developed, and where their remnants can be found in the Disney parks today.

So why write a book about the Walt Disney World that never was? A true understanding of the history of Walt Disney World must begin with the ideas that never came to be because, in many cases, those ideas morphed, changed, and evolved into the experiences that guests enjoy today. In addition, a recurring theme of Walt Disney Imagineering is that good ideas don't die. Therefore, an understanding of concepts that never came to be just might be a preview of things that are still to come.

It is also important to remember the wonderful work of Imagineers like Marc Davis, Claude Coats, and Harper Goff, whose contributions to the development of Disneyland and Walt Disney World are undeniable. We honor these brilliant artists not only by enjoying the attractions that they helped to create (such as the Haunted Mansion, Pirates of the Caribbean, and the Jungle Cruise), but also by remembering the unrealized concepts into which they put blood, sweat, and tears.

But who am I kidding? The most important reason why I wrote this book is because it was a lot of fun! What is more exciting for a Walt Disney World fan (other than actually riding attractions) than strolling through the parks, playing armchair Imagineer, and thinking about what could have been if these exciting ideas had actually made it into the parks? In other words, as a die-hard Walt Disney World fan, I wrote a book that I wanted to read, and I certainly hope that you agree.

This is a book about fire mountains and dragon towers, Persian resorts and animal carousels, progress cities and bullet trains, Mary Poppins and the Headless Horseman, Dick Tracy and Roger Rabbit. It is a book about grand ideas and legacies remembered. This is a book about the Walt Disney World that never was.

# The Happiest Definitions on Earth

In my legal practice, I spend a great deal of time drafting, reviewing, and revising contracts. One of the most important parts of any contract is the "definitions" section, where terms used frequently throughout a document are given a particular meaning. The purpose of adding a definitions section is to provide clarity to the document and to make it more efficient so as to prevent re-explaining what a particular term means each time it is used.

Walt Disney World has its own unique vocabulary that obsessed fans like me use and understand with ease. However, non-obsessed Disney fans may be less familiar with these terms, or understand them incompletely. The last thing I want to do is draw an analogy between this book (which I hope is extremely entertaining) and a contract (which most assuredly is not). However, at the risk of losing readers before they get to the first substantive (and fun!) chapter, I think it is a good idea to clarify the meanings of a few terms that will be used throughout the book:

**Cast Member** is the Disney term for employee. According to Disney, the company has no actual employees, but rather cast members who are performing on stage in front of guests at all times.

**Disneyland** is Disney's first theme park. It opened on July 17, 1955, in Anaheim, California.

**Disney's Animal Kingdom** is the fourth theme park that opened in Walt Disney World, on April 22, 1998. The park is devoted to animals—real, ancient, and imagined. At over five hundred acres in size, Animal Kingdom is also Disney's largest theme park.

**Disney's Hollywood Studios** is the third theme park that opened in Walt Disney World, on May 1, 1989. This park is devoted (at least at press time) to television, cinema, and all forms of entertainment. Hollywood Studios was originally known as the Disney-MGM Studios. The park was later renamed to Disney's Hollywood Studios when the Disney company's license with MGM was not renewed. Given the impending *Star Wars* and Pixar expansions, a new name for the park may be on the horizon.

**Epcot** is the second theme park that opened in Walt Disney World, on October 1, 1982. Epcot is devoted to human innovation, discovery, and culture. The term EPCOT was originally an acronym meaning Experimental Prototype Community of Tomorrow, the intended focus of the park when Walt Disney was alive. It was later named EPCOT Center when it opened to guests. The "Center" portion of the name was later dropped, and the lettering of Epcot is now in lowercase. (Unless it's essential to the narrative to do otherwise, I'll refer to the park consistently throughout the book as "Epcot.")

**Florida Project** is a reference to the covert acquisition of approximately forty square miles of land in central Florida by the Disney company, and the initial development of that land.

**Imagineers** are the artists, architects, animators, engineers, designers, mechanics, technicians, and musicians that create the Disney theme parks, lands, attractions, and experiences. The term is a combination of "imagination" and "engineers."

**Magic Kingdom** is the first theme park that opened in Walt Disney World, on October 1, 1971. It is the most popular theme park on the planet.

**The Walt Disney Company** (or more simply, the Disney company) is a multi-national corporation that, in addition to many other businesses, owns and runs the Walt Disney Studios and the Walt Disney Parks and Resorts (including Walt Disney World and Disneyland). The company has been known at different times as the Disney Brothers Cartoon Studio, The Walt Disney Studio, and Walt Disney Productions before assuming its current official name, The Walt Disney Company, in 1986. In this book, I'll refer to it as the Disney company, regardless of the time period being discussed.

**Walt Disney World** is the overarching term used to describe Disney's collection of theme parks, resort hotels, and other guest offerings in central Florida that originally opened to guests on October 1, 1971. Walt Disney World covers approximately twenty-seven thousand acres and today includes the Magic Kingdom, Epcot, Disney's Hollywood Studios, and Disney's Animal Kingdom.

**Wienie** is the term for a visual icon in the Disney theme parks that draws guests toward that icon's location. For example, Cinderella Castle, Space Mountain, and Big Thunder Mountain are all Magic Kingdom wienies. The term came from Walt himself who, upon arriving home from a hard day at work, would grab a wienie (or frankfurter) from the refrigerator to hold him over until dinner. His dog followed him everywhere, just as guests theoretically follow wienies in the Disney parks.

PART ONE

# Magic Kingdom

## Projects and Preliminary Concepts Abandoned

Costs of Projects and Preliminary Concepts Abandoned during the last three years represent a recognition, after evaluation, that certain projects in the concept and design stages which had been in work for varying periods of time had no foreseeable future use. It is a normal ongoing practice for the Company to dispense with all such work which has no immediately discernible future value. During 1976, these costs decreased by 53% because 1975 included the expensing, upon the completion of the first phase of Walt Disney World, of a number of projects in the concept and design stages which were determined to have no immediate foreseeable use.

—1976 Annual Report, Walt Disney Productions

## CHAPTER ONE

# Thunder Mesa

*We call them gag sessions. We get in there and toss ideas around. And we throw them in and put all the minds together and come up with something and say a little prayer and open it and hope it will go.*

— Walt Disney

If there was a Hall of Fame for Walt Disney World attractions that never came to be, Thunder Mesa would be the Babe Ruth, Michael Jordan, Muhammad Ali, and Bear Bryant entrants, rolled into one. Had it been constructed, Thunder Mesa would have been the most awe-inspiring and visually dominant theme park area in the Magic Kingdom, and home to an attraction in contention for the "best" in all of Disney World: the Western River Expedition.

Thunder Mesa was not an "attraction" per se, but a separate park area set within a massive show building themed as a Monument Valley mountain range in the heart of Frontierland. It would have housed numerous attractions and guest experiences, including a runaway mine train and a slap-stick indoor boat ride themed to the Old West.

Thunder Mesa has a long, tumultuous, captivating history filled with extensive plans, vast models, gorgeous artistic renderings, Imagineer squabbles, and eventually disappointment for the individual whose personal story goes hand-in-hand with that of his unrealized masterpiece: Marc Davis.

## Disney's Renaissance Man

Marc Davis' credits as both an animator in Disney feature films and as a designer and contributor to attractions and experiences in both Disneyland and Walt Disney World spanned more than four decades. His significant accomplishments earned him the distinction of being named a Disney Legend in 1989, an award that recognizes individuals who have made "an extraordinary and integral contribution to The Walt Disney Company." Marc Davis exemplified this standard perhaps better than anyone not named Disney.

Davis began work for Walt Disney in 1935 and became one of the legendary Nine Old Men, a moniker given to Walt's core group of animators during the mid 1930s through the 1950s. Davis' accomplishments as an animator are unparalleled. He designed and brought to life some of Disney's most beloved characters, including Snow White from *Snow White and the Seven Dwarfs* (1937); Bambi, Thumper, and Flower from *Bambi* (1942); Br'er Rabbit, Br'er Fox and Br'er Bear from the now controversial film *Song of the South* (1946); Mr. Toad, Rat, Mole, and MacBadger from *The Adventures of Ichabod and Mr. Toad* (1949); Cinderella and Prince Charming from *Cinderella* (1950); Alice from *Alice in Wonderland* (1950); Tinker Bell from *Peter Pan* (1953); and Aurora and Maleficent from *Sleeping Beauty* (1959). As is probably apparent from that impressive listing, Davis developed a reputation inside the Disney company (then known as Walt Disney Productions) as the "go-to" artist for noteworthy animated female characters.

In the 1960s, Davis' duties transitioned from an animator on Disney feature films to a designer and artist for Disney's new Anaheim theme park, Disneyland. Davis initially worked on projects such as the Mine Train Through Nature's Wonderland, a train ride experience set in the Old West, and The Enchanted Tiki Room, a tropical bird revue featuring audio-animatronic birds, flowers, and figures. Audio-animatronics was a groundbreaking new technology developed by Disney's Imagineers that created life-like robotic representations of people, animals, plants, and other objects.

Davis' most enduring contributions to the Disney theme parks are his work on Pirates of the Caribbean and The Haunted Mansion, two of the most beloved attractions in both Disney World and Disneyland. In each of these fan-favorite attractions, Davis inserted his signature brand of gags, jokes, and comical characters. The Davis touch provided a sense of humor and storytelling that made those experiences absolute classics and two of the most popular attractions at any theme park in the world.

In the words of Walt Disney himself, Marc Davis was a true "Renaissance man."

## Initial Plans

After the overwhelming success of Disneyland, which opened in 1955, Walt Disney began searching for locations across the country that might be suitable for similar theme park projects. One such location was St. Louis, Missouri. Disney began early stage plans for a St. Louis park that became known as the "Walt Disney's Riverfront Square" project. The proposed plan for Riverfront Square was unique in that it would have been entirely indoors.

In 1963, Davis developed preliminary plans for a Lewis and Clark-themed boat ride for Riverfront Square. This proposed attraction would have taken guests through landscapes and scenes from the famous explorers' travels and adventures, combining the elements of education and thrills with Davis' humor and comic relief. Ultimately, the Riverfront Square project in St. Louis fell through and, as a result, plans for Davis' Lewis and Clark boat attraction were temporarily shelved.

## Further Development

In the late 1960s, Davis was tasked with developing concepts and ideas for Disney's monumental Florida Project. He dusted off his plans for the Lewis and Clark attraction and revised them for a new boat ride experience that would transport guests through a hilarious and richly detailed Western landscape. Davis set a relatively small goal for himself: create the greatest attraction ever developed by the Disney company. In other words, he wanted to "out-pirate" his signature Pirates of the Caribbean. The attraction, the Western River Expedition, would be the key component of a larger theme park area located in the Frontierland section of the Magic Kingdom.

In order to gain a true understanding of how ambitious the Thunder Mesa project was, one must first grasp the sheer magnitude of the proposed show building. The massive structure was to be approximately four stories tall and cover a sprawling area from the current location of the Briar Patch gift shop (in front of Splash Mountain in Frontierland) all the way through the current footprint of the Big Thunder Mountain Railroad. It would have literally towered over Frontierland and provided a dramatic, breathtaking backdrop for that section of the park.

Given the immense size of the show building, it needed a convincing exterior façade to maintain thematic integrity with the rest of Frontierland. To address this concern, Davis planned on cloaking the show building with an immensely detailed Monument Valley-style mountain theme. Specifically, plans for Thunder Mesa called for a "table-top" mountain (otherwise known as a mesa) with a relatively flat summit that would create a dramatic vista and even more opportunities for guest entertainment. Even writing about it today, more than forty years since initial designs were created, I am amazed at how incredible the appearance of Thunder Mesa would have been.

Notably, Thunder Mesa was not an attraction, but instead an almost complete land unto itself, housing numerous attractions and guest experiences. Thunder Mesa would have included two signature attractions. First, guests would experience a runaway mine train attraction that travelled through a network of ore mines over, around, and through the mountainous landscape. The true star of Thunder Mesa, however, was to be the Western River Expedition.

## Western River Resources

The Western River Expedition would have been the centerpiece attraction for Thunder Mesa. We understand a great deal about the proposed ride experience for this attraction thanks to a number of different resources. First, a vast one-inch to one-foot scale model of the attraction was constructed in WED Enterprises (the Imagineering division of the Disney company that later became Walt Disney Imagineering) model shop, revealing the project in amazing scope and detail. According to some Imagineers, the Western River Expedition model was the most impressive, detailed, and, not surprisingly, one of the most expensive models they ever constructed.

In addition, Marc Davis and another Disney artist Mary Blair created an absolute treasure trove of detailed and humorous illustrations and renderings. Blair's amazing artistic contributions to Disney are headlined by her work on It's a Small World and the large Southwest diorama in the Grand Canyon Concourse lobby of the Contemporary Resort.

Other Walt Disney World experts such as Jim Hill (who published a detailed ten-part essay on Thunder Mesa over a decade ago) and Mike Lee also wrote richly detailed and thoroughly entertaining accounts of the Western River Expedition experience. And another Disney Imagineer, Tony Baxter, provided a fascinating presentation on the ride-through experience for the Western River Expedition at the D23 (the official Disney fan club) conference held in 2011. As we will soon see, Baxter has his own controversial connection to both Thunder Mesa and the Western River Expedition.

## A Western River Ride-Through

What follows is a general description of the ride-through experience for the Western River Expedition. No one can know what the attraction would have been like with 100% accuracy, as the plans for it changed, morphed, and evolved over time. But based on the above resources, and more, we do understand many of the key components.

Guests would first enter Thunder Mesa through a cave, leading to a canyon set in perpetual twilight with stars twinkling high above. I imagine an interior environment similar to the Mexico Pavilion in Epcot's World Showcase, only with a more dramatic effect. Guests would then arrive at a dock before loading into their ride vehicles, which in this case would have been boats similar to those used in Pirates of the Caribbean and It's a Small World.

The narrator and star of the attraction was a colorful audio-animatronic owl named Hoot Gibson. After Hoot provided the safety spiel, the ride would begin. The boats first travelled "up" a waterfall before beginning a peaceful and gentle float down a calm river. Clouds projected on the ceiling would resemble cowboys, cattle and other Western-themed characters, animals, and objects.

One of the many colorful illustrations of the Western River Expedition depicts a scene featuring colorful dime store novels with comical images like Davey Crockett boxing a bear and Annie Oakley posing with her rifle. These novels would have set the tone for the humorous scenes yet to come.

The boats would next enter a cavern full of stalactites and stalagmites. As Imagineer Tony Baxter explained during his 2011 D23 presentation, these rock and mineral formations would take the shape of animals and people, including an old man and a cowboy. One can only imagine how captivating this effect could have been with proper lighting and music.

The boats would then enter a colorful Western scene featuring a variety of audio-animatronic animals including buffaloes and prairie dogs. Among the funny sights and sounds is a singing cowboy sitting on horseback while serenading an audience of steers to the attraction's theme song, with both the horse and the steers singing back to him. Even a series of desert cacti would join in on the comical vocalization.

Next, guests would pass a horde of bandits robbing a stagecoach. The bandits would be dressed, of all things, like a mariachi band. As depicted in another piece of beautiful conceptual artwork, the sinister bandits wear striking red bandanas to mask their faces, as do their horses. Luckily, guests would pass the bandits unscathed...for the time being at least.

The boats would then enter the town of Dry Gulch, my personal favorite scene of the entire attraction. Thanks to several pieces of breathtaking artwork by Marc Davis and Mary Blair, Disney fans are able to see this tableaux in fantastic detail. More than any other, these scenes reveal how fantastic the Western River Expedition could have been in real life.

It is clear from the illustrations that the setting is "after hours," with cowboys and women drinking, dancing, and having all manner of rowdy fun. Perhaps the most famous, and humorous, depiction of the Western River Expedition is a scene from Dry Gulch of a boisterous cowboy and his horse who have managed to get on top of a saloon's roof. It appears as though the cowboy had a few drinks before exiting the saloon, as he has a large smile on his face and is firing his six-shooters haphazardly into the air. Of course, not every citizen of Dry Gulch is happy about the mischievous fun, as some of the more straight-laced residents look on with disapproval.

The action picks up ahead as a group of bank robbers engage in a massive shootout with the local sheriff and numerous concerned citizens. One armed resident peeks out of the second floor of a barn, while another cowboy positions himself behind a water wagon that has been hit by several bullets, as evidenced by water pouring through numerous bullet holes. A man with shaving cream still slathered on his face stands on the front porch of Al's Tonsorial Parlor and aims his gun down the street. The town mortician eerily peeks out his door with a deadly grin, no doubt considering the uptick in business this chaos will bring. It is an action-packed sequence. Fortunately, guests are able to sail past the chaos unscathed and pass underneath a bridge.

Guests would hear the pounding of drums as they entered the next scene, a Native American diorama with a marvelous painted desert backdrop. Several members of the tribe are seen atop a flat butte performing a rain dance, which is all too effective as rain pours down upon the entirety of the rock. A comedic trio of coyotes howls at a fire and a medicine man performs a strange ritual while a buxom Native American beauty observes. A lightning bolt eventually sets the surrounding forest ablaze, as the gentle river upon which guests are travelling quickly intensifies and turns into dangerous rapids.

As if things could not get worse, the bandits from the beginning of the attraction have finally caught up to the boats. A detailed 1968 sketch labeled "BANDITS (AT TOP OF DOWN RAMP)" for the "WESTERN RIVER RIDE" provides a wonderful illustration of this scene. On the right side of the river are three bandits on horseback, all with six-shooters in hand. On the left of the river are two additional bandits on horseback, including the presumed leader wearing a distinctive sombrero with a guitar on his back and six-shooters at the ready. The beady eyes peering over the red bandannas worn by the bandits and their horses make it clear that this is a group of sinister scoundrels. The bandits, not surprisingly, demand that guests turn over their possessions. When the guests refuse...it is over the falls they go!

At this point guests finally reach the climax of the Western River Expedition as their boats cascade down a waterfall and outside of the show building. The boats would then circle back into the interior of Thunder Mesa and return to the load/unload areas.

The Western River Expedition would have relied on two essential storytelling elements. First, there would have been a heavy emphasis on music. Noted Disney songwriter Buddy Baker (whose other attraction song credits include the Haunted Mansion and If You Had Wings) penned the attraction's theme music, which would have been played in different tones and styles throughout the experience (similar to the Haunted Mansion's theme song, Grim Grinning Ghosts) and sang by a variety of animals, people, and plants.

A second important attribute of the Western River Expedition was that it would have had an enormous amount of audio-animatronic figures: approximately one hundred and fifty! In comparison, Pirates of the Caribbean in Disneyland, which was known for its large number of audio-animatronics, had around one hundred such figures. Work even began on putting these numerous figures into production.

## A Runaway Mine Train, Walking Trails, and Pack Mules

Although the Western River Expedition was to be the centerpiece of Thunder Mesa, plans for the project also included a second headliner attraction in the form of a runaway mine train that would race over, around, and through the mountain. Guests would board vintage ore carts that would take them on a scenic tour of the Mesa's mining operations. The mine train attraction would start quietly and peacefully before, not unexpectedly, experiencing problems that increase in intensity before reaching the attraction's climax, where guests narrowly avoid a disastrous fall down a bottomless pit.

Plans for the Thunder Mesa mine train were significant because the attraction would have been the first "thrill" ride and the first roller coaster at Walt Disney World. In his book *Dream It! Do It!* (2013), Imagineer Marty Sklar described the decision of not including thrill rides in the Magic Kingdom on opening day as one of the biggest "goofs" of Disney Imagineers, noting that "we figured there would be too many older, retired people." With that belief, the attractions in operation on the Magic Kingdom's opening day were largely family-centered, and included classics such as Peter Pan's Flight, Tropical Serenade (which later became Walt Disney's Enchanted Tiki Room), Jungle Cruise, Country Bear Jamboree, Haunted Mansion, and Hall of Presidents. While all of these attractions were entertaining, none of them could be described as exhilarating.

Disneyland's popular roller coaster, the Matterhorn Bobsleds, was not replicated in Walt Disney World. Space Mountain would not open until 1975, and Thunder Mesa's mountainous descendants, Big Thunder Mountain Railroad and Splash Mountain, would not open until 1980 and 1992, respectively.

In connection with the thrill-ride experience, the mine train would have included an exciting backwards descent through the interior of the Thunder Mesa show building in almost complete darkness. If that sounds familiar, then you have probably ridden Expedition Everest in Animal Kingdom, which opened in 2006. Perhaps the most adrenaline-pumping portion of the Everest coaster is its backwards descent.

In addition to the two headliner attractions, Thunder Mesa would have also offered guests intricately themed walking trails that would lead through a variety of desert vegetation to the "table-top" peak of Thunder Mesa. At the summit, not only would guests be able to experience perhaps the most amazing views in all of the Magic Kingdom, they would also see a Pueblo Indian Village, enjoy pack mule rides across the butte, and enjoy Southwest-themed shopping, dining, and entertainment options.

## Promotional Materials, Coming Soon, and Phase One

In 1969, Disney issued a booklet entitled "A Complete Edition About Walt Disney World" that provided a preview of "The Vacation Kingdom of the World." This booklet emphasized those attractions that would be unique to Walt Disney World, and not simply replications of pre-existing Disneyland experiences. The Disney World "original" attractions depicted in the booklet included Space Mountain, Swiss Family Isle (which eventually became the Swiss Family Tree House), Hall of Presidents, and the Country Bear Band (which later became Country Bear Jamboree). What is interesting in regard to the Thunder Mesa project is that the "Complete Edition" included concept artwork for not only Thunder Mesa as a whole, but also a second picture specifically for the Western River Expedition. It is clear that in 1969, Thunder Mesa was an important project for Walt Disney World.

Another reference to Thunder Mesa was included in the 1969 Annual Report to the shareholders and employees of Walt Disney Productions. This report included a picture of Marc Davis working on a model for the Western River Expedition, with the following caption:

> WESTERN RIVER EXPEDITION: Project Designer Marc Davis completes a model for this musical parody of the wild old west. On the grand scale of Disneyland's "Pirates of the Caribbean," the attraction will be located in "Thunder Mesa."

In addition to the "Complete Edition" and the 1969 Annual Report, a famous depiction of Thunder Mesa appeared as concept artwork on a Disney World pre-opening day postcard. The postcard depicts park guests gazing across a waterway at a vast mountainous backdrop. Although it is difficult to discern specific details about Thunder Mesa from this postcard, two waterfall exit paths and a small town appear in the illustration.

In 1970, Disney issued another colorful marketing booklet, this one named "Preview Edition Walt Disney World 'The Vacation Kingdom of the World.'" As you would expect, the booklet provided beautiful artistic renderings and detailed descriptions of the various resorts, amenities, and entertainment offerings that were coming soon to the massive Florida Project. It also provided readers with an entertaining preview of the various attractions and experiences guests could expect at the Magic Kingdom, broken down for each of its six theme park lands.

The "Preview Edition" provided this description of Thunder Mesa:

> Another major attraction to be added during Walt Disney World's "Phase One" is Thunder Mesa, which will tower high above dense pine forests, offering a spectacular panoramic view of Frontierland. Resembling a "table-top" mountain, typical of those found on Southwestern deserts, it would include a pueblo-style village and a series of exciting adventures. Inside Thunder Mesa, guests will "sign aboard" the Western River Expedition—a musical parody of the wild old West. On their cruise, they'll come face to face with cowboys and Indians in a frontier fantasy on the grand scale of Disneyland's famous Pirates of the Caribbean.

The "Preview Edition" explained the "Phase One" terminology as being Disney's plan for the addition of various hotels, recreation options, entertainment experiences, and theme park attractions during the first five years of Walt Disney World.

Because Thunder Mesa was such a monumental project, it carried with it a monumental price tag. As construction for the Magic Kingdom progressed and costs began to soar, Disney executives faced a difficult decision. Did they move forward with the ambitious Thunder Mesa project and sacrifice multiple other attractions? Or did they devote resources to developing numerous smaller attractions to help divert and occupy the huge volume of theme park guests expected on opening day? Ultimately, Disney chose the second option, and Thunder Mesa was placed on the Phase One list.

The rationale behind a Phase One plan for Thunder Mesa, as opposed to pushing that it be completed for opening day, was threefold. First, the five-year Phase One period provided Disney personnel with sufficient time to get a threshold number of attractions and offerings operating at the Magic Kingdom to address the expected crowd levels. Second, the revenue from the Magic Kingdom, which was expected to be significant, could be used to offset the enormous construction costs for Thunder Mesa. Finally, a promise of additional attractions coming within a five-year period was the perfect enticement for first time visitors (which they all were at that point) to come back to Disney World in the future.

Notwithstanding the Phase One delay, a "Fun Map" prepared in 1971 by Paul Hartley presented a very light-hearted, colorful, and not-to-scale depiction of the Magic Kingdom and the surrounding Bay Lake, Seven Seas Lagoon, and resort hotels. To the far left of this Fun Map is a large depiction of Thunder Mesa as a mountainous landscape through which the Magic Kingdom Railroad passed.

It's clear that, despite delaying the construction of Thunder Mesa, there was no doubt that it would ultimately be built as a part of the Disney company's Phase One plans.

## Where Are the Pirates?

Pirates of the Caribbean opened in Disneyland on March 18, 1967, and quickly became one of the most popular attractions in the park. Thanks both to the positive reactions by guests at Disneyland and the promotion of Pirates on Disney's immensely popular weekly television program *Walt Disney's Wonderful World of Color*, the attraction became a nationwide phenomenon. For theme park fans across the country, an opportunity to ride Pirates of the Caribbean became a rite of passage.

When planning for the Magic Kingdom, Disney executive leadership, in particular Dick Irvine, the executive vice president and chief operations officer of WED Enterprises, wanted to mix popular attractions from Disneyland with new and exciting projects unique to Disney World. The 1970 "Preview Edition" made a point to emphasize this approach, noting that "[w]hile some of the attractions in the new Magic Kingdom will be familiar to the more than 90 million people who have already visited Disneyland, many more will be unique to this new Disney theme park in Florida."

Of course, the decision of which Disneyland concepts to bring to Disney World was difficult. A delicate balance needed to be struck between capitalizing on the vast goodwill created by Disneyland while also providing enough unique offerings to entice guests to make the trip to Florida.

Irvine and the rest of the Disney decision-makers did incorporate many familiar attractions from Disneyland into the Disney World opening day plans, including what would become known as Walt Disney's Enchanted Tiki Room, the Jungle Cruise, and Peter Pan's Flight. Given the popularity of Pirates of the Caribbean on the West Coast, it would most assuredly be one of the attractions replicated in Florida...right?

Surprisingly, Disney executives made the decision to NOT include Pirates of the Caribbean in Walt Disney World. As crazy as this decision may sound from today's perspective, Disney did have a couple of reasons for making it. First, because Florida was so close in geographic proximity to the actual Caribbean, Disney executives worried that guest excitement and anticipation would not be high for a pirate-based attraction. In fact, Disney made clear in its 1970 Annual Report that it expected guests to visit Disney World in conjunction with trips to the Caribbean:

> Walt Disney World is by definition a destination point, a place where people will come from afar and where they will stay for several days in combination with a visit to the Florida and Caribbean area.

In addition to the geographic proximity concern, construction costs for Disney World were astronomical...and growing. As Pirates was one of the most expensive attractions in Disneyland, the cost of adding the fan favorite to the Magic Kingdom would have been a budgeting nightmare. Finally, as noted by author Jason Surrell in *Pirates of the Caribbean, From the Magic Kingdom to the Movies* (2005), construction of Pirates in Florida would have been at the cost of several other attractions that were needed to "eat guests" and deal with the expected flood of theme park visitors. Ironically, this final point was also a key justification for delaying Thunder Mesa to the Phase One timeline.

You can probably guess what happened when the Magic Kingdom opened pirate-less on October 1, 1971. Thousands of guests began asking one question over and over again: "Where are the pirates?!?" Unhappy pirate-seekers wrote nasty complaint letters, made angry phone calls to guest relations, and continually registered complaints with cast members in the park.

Demand for Pirates of the Caribbean was so significant that in 1972 the president of Walt Disney Productions, E. Cardon "Card" Walker, decided to give guests what they wanted. Walker tasked Imagineers with creating a Walt Disney World version of Pirates of the Caribbean on a breakneck timeline. The Imagineers tried to explain to Card that they were already working on a boat ride attraction that would "out-pirate" Pirates, but Walker had made up his mind and there was no convincing him otherwise. A site was selected for Pirates of the Caribbean in Adventureland and construction began in the fall of 1972. In an attempt to stop the repeated "Where are the pirates?" questions, cast members even began wearing buttons that stated, "The Pirates are Coming! Christmas 1973."

To add insult to injury, it was Marc Davis who was in large part tasked with designing the Magic Kingdom version of Pirates of the Caribbean. Placed in a very precarious situation, Davis at the very least wanted the opportunity to improve upon his work from the Disneyland version of Pirates. Unfortunately, because of several factors, including time, cost, and geographic constraints within the park, Davis was forced to shorten the experience rather than expand it. Davis was not happy, but nonetheless completed his work on the abbreviated Pirates of the Caribbean project while holding out hope that Thunder Mesa and the Western River Expedition would still be constructed.

Pirates of the Caribbean opened in the Adventureland section of Walt Disney World on December 15, 1973. It quickly became one of the most beloved and popular attractions in the entire park, and remains so today.

## A Collection of Problems

There is no doubt that the decision to build Pirates of the Caribbean was a tremendous blow to Thunder Mesa's hopes of being constructed. The area reserved for Thunder Mesa was right next door to Pirates of the

Caribbean, and its key component, the Western River Expedition, was a Western-version of Pirates. Given these issues, the thought of expending the significant amount of money and resources necessary to build Thunder Mesa caused many Disney executives to question the feasibility of moving forward with the project.

On December 20, 1971, less than three months after the Magic Kingdom's opening day, Roy O. Disney passed away. As Roy was one of the biggest supporters for the Western River Expedition, his death not only robbed the Disney company of an amazing man, it also robbed the Western River Expedition of one of its strongest advocates.

The massive projected costs of Thunder Mesa, which initially led to it being placed on the Phase One plan, continued to play a critical role in hurting the project. By 1972, there were multiple projects on the horizon for Disney World's Magic Kingdom, including a much-needed expansion of Tomorrowland with the addition of Space Mountain, the WEDWay PeopleMover, the Starjets, and Walt Disney's Carousel of Progress. Given these economic pressures, Card Walker began making cost-cutting suggestions for Davis' project, such as utilizing the molds that were used to sculpt the faces of the characters in Pirates of the Caribbean instead of sculpting entirely new molds for the Thunder Mesa characters. As desperate as Davis was to have his masterpiece constructed, he still rejected this proposal outright.

Another economic roadblock to Thunder Mesa came in the form of the energy crisis of the early 1970s. When the OPEC restricted sales of oil to the West, gas prices in the United States skyrocketed. Since thousands of guests travelled to Disney World by car, these restrictions on oil sales had a tremendous negative impact on the number of people willing to incur that increased expense to make the trip to Florida. As a result, theme park attendance plummeted. Card Walker responded by tightening the Disney belt even further. Not surprisingly, projects like Thunder Mesa were once again postponed.

Aside from the construction of Pirates of the Caribbean, the loss of Roy Disney, excessive costs, and a negative economic environment, Thunder Mesa also faced a significant cultural issue in the early 1970s that also threatened its viability. As discussed above, the artistic renderings of Thunder Mesa and in particular the Western River Expedition were rich in detail and humorous in their portrayal of a journey through the Old West. Unfortunately, the depiction of Native Americans in those drawings featured a number of politically incorrect stereotypes. These included large noses, beady eyes, and alcohol consumption for the male Native American characters, and vivacious and buxom bodies for the females. Disney fans may recognize some of these same characteristics in the portrayal of

Native Americans in the Disney classic film, *Peter Pan*, but the difference in the scrutiny between *Peter Pan* and the renderings for Thunder Mesa were obvious. *Peter Pan* was released in 1953, while Davis' Thunder Mesa depictions were produced in the 1970s, a much different time in terms of political correctness and sensitivity.

Davis claimed that there was no ill will or prejudice at work in his drawings, as all of the characters depicted therein were exaggerated versions of reality (including the cowboys). The goal was to create laughs, not make political statements. Nevertheless, these political pressures clearly affected Davis and the plans for the Western River Expedition. One of the early concept paintings for Western River Expedition depicted a "Magical Elixir Wagon," where a travelling medicine man advertised his various offerings to a crowd. The original version included several Native American characters. However, a later version of the illustration removed the Native Americans and replaced them with a Caucasian strong man.

Notwithstanding these numerous hurdles, in 1973 the Western River Expedition became a central part of a twenty-three minute film called *The Walt Disney Story* about Walt's life, from his childhood in Marceline, Missouri, to his death in 1966. The post-show area for *The Walt Disney Story* was regularly used to preview coming attractions and lands for Disney World. In 1973, this area showed a portion of the model for the Western River Expedition and advertised the attraction as "coming soon." It also included an audio-animatronic version of Hoot Gibson, the owl who was to serve as the narrator for the attraction. When guests pressed a button, Hoot awoke from his slumber and invited guests to come back soon to see the Western River Expedition for themselves.

## Tony Baxter and Big Thunder Mountain Railroad

With construction of Pirates of the Caribbean complete, and Marc Davis' hopes to salvage some portion of Thunder Mesa dwindling, the impact of another Disney Imagineer, Tony Baxter, delivered the death knell to the concept's hopes of ever becoming a reality.

Tony Baxter was much younger than Marc Davis, and is perhaps the most famous of the so-called second generation of Disney Imagineers. Baxter grew up in California, and worked his way from literally sweeping the floors in Disneyland to selling ice cream, and eventually to working at WED Enterprises following his graduation from California State University. Baxter's numerous creative contributions to Disney include, in addition to Big Thunder Mountain Railroad, 20,000 Leagues Under the Sea, Splash

Mountain, Star Tours, Journey into Imagination with Figment, and the Finding Nemo Submarine Voyage.

Baxter spent considerable time working on the above-mentioned model for Thunder Mesa. It sat in the Imagineering model shop until 1974 when Card Walker discovered it during a visit to the shop. After a discussion with Baxter about his comments and criticisms of the Thunder Mesa plans, Walker instructed Baxter to draw up plans for an independent mine train attraction, separate and apart from the plans for Thunder Mesa. The Baxter stand-alone project was eventually green-lit by Disney executives for inclusion in Disneyland. This approval also included a version of the attraction for Walt Disney World.

The 1972 Annual Report of Walt Disney Productions set forth several new attraction ideas, including a conceptual depiction of "Big Thunder Railway" which was described as a "high-speed western adventure." The 1972 Annual Report also made clear that this would "be the first step toward the completion of Thunder Mesa."

Groundbreaking for the Big Thunder Mountain Railroad in Walt Disney World took place on January 15, 1979, while the Disneyland version was still under construction. The massive project took twenty-two months to complete and used six-hundred-and-thirty tons of steel! The construction cost of Big Thunder Mountain was approximately $17 million, including $300 thousand worth of authentic mining equipment used to adorn the Big Thunder queue and attraction. The end result is a Magic Kingdom "wienie" that stands almost two hundred feet tall, towering over the landscape of Frontierland. Big Thunder Mountain Railroad officially opened on November 15, 1980. As was the case with Pirates of the Caribbean, Big Thunder Mountain was an immediate success and remains one of the most popular attractions in the Magic Kingdom. However, its appearance was yet another tremendous blow to the hopes that Thunder Mesa would ever come to fruition.

You are probably wondering how Marc Davis reacted to Baxter's concept for a separate Big Thunder Mountain attraction, so similar to that of the Thunder Mesa runaway train ride. Well, it was not good. By all reports, Davis was furious with Baxter and carried this resentment with him for the rest of his life.

For his own part, Baxter felt terrible about the situation. He even created a plan that would have allowed for the remainder of the Thunder Mesa concept to be constructed adjacent to the Big Thunder Mountain Railroad (even though the prospects for that idea actually working were probably very small). Notwithstanding these efforts, it does not appear that Davis was ever able to forgive Baxter for the wrongs Davis perceived had taken place.

## No Official Word

In 1975, the Disney company announced that its Phase One plan was complete. This was terrible news for Marc Davis and Thunder Mesa, as everyone inside of Disney knew that Phase Two would focus on making Walt's dream for Epcot a reality.

The model of the Western River Expedition displayed in the post-show area of *The Walt Disney Story* was literally walled up and forgotten, and poor Hoot Gibson re-focused his promotional activities on Epcot.

Interestingly enough, there was never an actual announcement that either Thunder Mesa or the Western River Expedition had been scrapped. After releasing so many different materials announcing the impending arrival of Thunder Mesa, many Disney guests were looking forward to experiencing this massive Frontierland addition. Rather than making an official announcement and drawing the ire of these disappointed fans, Disney did... nothing. They just never built it.

## The Legacy of Thunder Mesa Today

Although neither Thunder Mesa nor Western River Expedition ever made it into Disney World, there are a few tributes and fun artifacts found in the parks today that pay homage to the never-realized Davis masterpiece.

The Big Thunder Mountain Railroad is the most obvious tribute, as it evolved directly from the runaway mine train component of Thunder Mesa. In 2012, Disney announced an entirely new backstory for the Big Thunder Mountain Railroad. As a part of this theming revitalization, the interior queue was also updated, providing numerous gags and details that greatly enrich the experience. Several of these queue updates reference Thunder Mesa. For example, the land grant for Barnabus T. Bullion on which Big Thunder Mountain sits is in "the Western River Valley." Also, an advertisement for the Butterfly Stage Line's Gateway to the West includes rates for a trip from Thunder Mesa to Rainbow Ridge (the name of the town in Disneyland's version of Big Thunder Mountain). A crate in the queue is labeled Western River Explosives: 40% Strength, another nod to the Western River Expedition. Finally, a "fusing cage" includes tributes to numerous Disney Imagineers, including a listing for Matchstick Marc, a long overdue reference to Marc Davis.

Guests who have experienced the Living with the Land attraction in Epcot's Future World have also seen pieces of the Western River Expedition, although they probably did not realize it. In the prairie scene of the attraction, immediately before guests arrive at the farmhouse, they see a buffalo and several prairie dogs. These mechanical animals were constructed for use in the Western River Expedition and were placed into storage before being retrieved and used as part of Living with the Land.

Frontierland did eventually get an indoor boat ride attraction that floats by several audio-animatronic dioramas before eventually falling down a large waterfall when Splash Mountain opened in 1992. It was the brainchild of none other than Tony Baxter. In another interesting twist, rumor has it that during the construction of Splash Mountain in Disneyland, costs soared well beyond projected budgets. In order to save money, many of the audio-animatronic figures in the Disneyland version of Splash Mountain were "pirated" from America Sings, a less-than-popular Disneyland attraction that featured a host of audio-animatronic critters. In a cruel bit of irony, it just so happens that America Sings was another project close to the heart of its creator, Marc Davis.

In addition to the Magic Kingdom, the legacy of Thunder Mesa and Western River Expedition continues to live on in Disney parks throughout the world. For example, in Tokyo Disneyland the theme park's train is named the Western River Railroad, and Disneyland Paris includes both a Thunder Mesa Riverboat Landing and a Thunder Mesa Mercantile Building.

## Final Take

Thunder Mesa would have been amazing—that much is clear from the artwork that Disney fans can still enjoy today. For me, wishing that Thunder Mesa and the Western River Expedition had been completed is bittersweet. On the one hand, the thought of a towering mountainous landscape looming over Frontierland with a Western version of Pirates of the Caribbean is almost too good to resist. On the other hand, Big Thunder Mountain Railroad, Splash Mountain, and Pirates of the Caribbean are three of my favorite attractions that, depending on the circumstances, might not have been developed had Davis' project been realized.

Marc Davis died on January 12, 2000, in Glendale, California. From Snow White to Cinderella, Bambi to Br'er Rabbit, Tinker Bell to Maleficent, and Pirates of the Caribbean to the Haunted Mansion, Disney fans around the world will always remember Davis' immense contributions and legacy. Just make sure that the next time you walk through Frontierland on your way to the Big Thunder Mountain Railroad with a jumbo turkey leg in hand, you tip your hat to Davis and take a few minutes to think about what could have been if his dream of Thunder Mesa had come true.

CHAPTER TWO

# Lost Fantasyland Dark Rides

*Fantasyland is dedicated to the young and the young-at-heart—to those who believe that when you wish upon a star, your dreams do come true.*

—Walt Disney

Walt Disney's initial inspiration for Disneyland was to create an environment where the entire family could spend the day laughing, playing, and having fun together. Of all the different theme park "lands" represented in Walt Disney World, Fantasyland is the clearest embodiment of that ideal.

On the Magic Kingdom's opening day, October 1, 1971, Fantasyland featured a variety of attractions that the whole family could enjoy together, including Dumbo the Flying Elephant, the Mad Tea Party, Cinderella's Golden Carrousel (now known as the Prince Charming Regal Carrousel), and It's a Small World. Fantasyland also included three popular dark rides: Snow White's Adventures (later Snow White's Scary Adventures), Peter Pan's Flight, and Mr. Toad's Wild Ride. The term "dark ride" is used to describe an indoor attraction where ride vehicles take guests on a predetermined route through different scenes of a story, with a combination of audio-animatronics, lighting, music, and other Imagineering effects used to tell that story and focus guests' attention on specific areas.

Unbeknownst to most Disney fans, initial plans for Disney World's Fantasyland called for a completely different set of dark rides than what eventually opened with the Magic Kingdom in 1971. These proposed attractions were based on the classic Disney films *Sleeping Beauty* (1959), *Mary Poppins* (1964), *The Adventures of Ichabod and Mr. Toad* (1949), and *The Sword in the Stone* (1963), and would have offered unique and original experiences not already featured in California's Disneyland.

## *Sleeping Beauty* and *Snow White*

*Snow White and the Seven Dwarfs* is a cinematic masterpiece. Released in 1937, it was the first full-length animated feature film and the beginning of a Disney animated film legacy that continues today. *Snow White* was so significant that Walt Disney was awarded an honorary Oscar for the film, which featured a classic Oscar statue and seven smaller Oscar figures beside it.

Because of the significance of *Snow White* to both the Disney company and the film industry as a whole, it made sense that the Magic Kingdom would include a ride based on this monumental film. However, Disney executives wanted to strike a balance between replicating attractions that already existed in Disneyland and creating new concepts for Disney World. This balance was reflected in the 1968 Annual Report for Walt Disney Productions:

> Although many attractions will be familiar to the 76 million people who have already visited California's Disneyland, many more will be unique to the new theme park in Walt Disney World.

Disneyland already featured an attraction based on *Snow White*. Not wanting to repeat themselves, Disney executives instead considered adding an attraction based on *Sleeping Beauty* in the Florida version of Fantasyland.

*Sleeping Beauty* was released in 1959 and, while widely considered a Disney classic today, was not the overwhelming box office hit that Disney hoped it would be. Nevertheless, a dark ride featuring a beautiful princess, entertaining fairies, and perhaps the most famous Disney villain of all, Maleficent, made for an exciting attraction idea.

The proposed *Sleeping Beauty* dark ride would have taken guests through various tableaus from the 1959 film before ultimately encountering Maleficent in her ominous fire-breathing dragon form. Although Sleeping Beauty Castle served as the visual centerpiece for Disneyland, the park did not have an actual *Sleeping Beauty* dark ride. Therefore, a *Sleeping Beauty* attraction in the Magic Kingdom would have been an original.

## *Mary Poppins* and *Peter Pan*

Strange as it may seem today, Imagineers also considered developing an attraction based on *Mary Poppins* instead of the Fantasyland fan-favorite Peter Pan's Flight.

*Peter Pan*, Disney's fourteenth animated film, was released in 1953 to a positive critical response. The film, based upon J.M. Barrie's classic story of the same name, was notably the last animated film on which Walt Disney's legendary Nine Old Men group of animators worked together.

Given the child-centered story of *Peter Pan*, the boy who never grew up, a *Pan*-based attraction in Walt Disney World's Fantasyland made perfect sense. However, as was the case with *Snow White*, a *Peter Pan* attraction already existed in Disneyland. Therefore, Imagineers considered incorporating an attraction based on the film *Mary Poppins* into the Magic Kingdom.

*Mary Poppins* was released in 1964 and is considered by many to be the greatest Disney movie ever made. Based on the book series by P.L. Travers, *Mary Poppins* combined live-action actors, animated characters, and a series of upbeat songs to create a classic family film that endures even today. The film featured incredible performances by Julie Andrews and Dick Van Dyke, and was nominated for thirteen Academy Awards, including Best Picture. The film won five of those Academy Awards, including a Best Actress nod for Andrews and Best Original Song for "Chim Chim Cher-ee."

The proposed *Mary Poppins* attraction would have recreated one of the more memorable scenes from the film, as guests would have ridden turn-of-the century style merry-go-round horses through Bert's chalk drawings en route to a joyous journey through various dioramas of English landscapes, including a fox hunt and a horserace. The attraction would have been a "jolly holiday" experience with appearances by the stars of the film, Mary Poppins and Bert. An alternate version called for umbrella-style ride vehicles that would take guests across numerous London rooftops.

Regardless of which version the Imagineers might have chosen, one can only imagine how wonderful the theme music would have been with so many beautiful options available from the film, including "A Spoonful of Sugar," "Jolly Holliday," and my personal favorite, "Chim Chim Cher-ee."

## Ichabod Crane, Merlin, and Mr. Toad

Imagineers also strongly considered, in lieu of Mr. Toad's Wild Ride, an attraction based on "The Legend of Sleepy Hollow." This is especially interesting due to the close connection between Mr. Toad and "The Legend of Sleepy Hollow," from the 1949 Disney animated film *The Adventures of Ichabod and Mr. Toad.*

This film consisted of two segments based on the 1908 novel *The Wind in the Willows* by Kenneth Grahame and Washington Irving's 1820 short story "The Legend of Sleepy Hollow," respectively. *The Adventures of Ichabod and Mr. Toad* represented the eleventh animated feature film released by Disney. It was also the last of Disney's "packaged" films that became popular during the World War II era because of their lower costs as compared to full-length animated films. It followed *Saludos Amigos* (1942), *The Three Caballeros* (1945), *Make Mine Music* (1946), *Fun and Fancy Free* (1947), and *Melody Time* (1948).

*The Adventures of Ichabod and Mr. Toad* featured the work of famed Disney animators and members of Walt's Nine Old Men Frank Thomas, Ollie Johnston, John Lounsbery, Wolfgang Reitherman, Milt Kahl, and Ward Kimball. Bing Crosby provided the masterful narration for the Sleepy Hollow portion of the film, along with the voices of Ichabod Crane and Brom Bones. English Actor Eric Blore provided the voice of J. Thaddeus Toad, Esq., the star of the Toad segment.

As was the case with *Snow White* and *Peter Pan*, a Toad-based attraction already existed in Disneyland in the form of Mr. Toad's Wild Ride. Therefore, Imagineers contemplated a new attraction based on Irving's famous short story.

The proposed Sleepy Hollow attraction would have included hollowed-out jack-o-lantern ride vehicles that would take guests through the eerie rural landscape of Tarrytown, New York, the real-life setting for "The Legend of Sleepy Hollow." As you might imagine, guests would eventually encounter the star of the attraction, the ominous Headless Horseman. Although the concept does seem a bit out of place for the theme of Fantasyland, and would probably have been more appropriate in Liberty Square, a Sleepy Hollow-based attraction would certainly have provided both fun and thrills for theme park guests.

Interestingly enough, Imagineers also considered an attraction based on the 1963 Disney animated film *The Sword in the Stone* in place of Mr. Toad's Wild Ride. The attraction would have featured a wizard's duel, as depicted in the film, with sage old wizard Merlin engaged in a magical battle with the notorious sorceress Madam Mim. Guests would have found themselves in the middle of the battle, narrowly escaping a variety of magical spells being hurled between Merlin and Mim. Given the medieval setting of *The Sword in the Stone*, an attraction based on that film seemed like a natural fit given the equally medieval setting of Fantasyland itself, which is set behind the majestic towers of Cinderella Castle.

## Cutting Costs and Concepts

As is the case with many grand ideas that never came to be, financial pressures eventually led to the Sleeping Beauty, Mary Poppins, Sleepy Hollow, and Sword in the Stone concepts being cancelled. During the late 1960s and early 1970s, Walt Disney World was the largest private construction project in the world. As both the scope and the costs for the Florida Project soared, executives, and in particular Roy O. Disney, began looking for ways to save money. In his letter to shareholders entitled "A WORD FROM ROY O. DISNEY" that accompanied the 1970 Annual Report for Walt Disney Productions, Roy explained the growing costs for the Florida Project:

> In the beginning, we planned for the [Magic Kingdom] to accommodate 8 million guests annually, but we now feel that estimate was too conservative, and we are planning the park to handle a 10 million visitor load. This increased scope has necessitated the addition of several rides and the expansion of others, which, in turn, has given rise to some substantial additional costs....
>
> For these reasons, it now appears that our early estimate of corporate investment is going to be substantially exceeded.

Because of this financial pressure, Disney executives made the decision to save the increased cost and expense that would be required to develop new attraction concepts. Instead, Disney knew that it already had three attractions that were popular with theme park guests in Disneyland. Disney executives also believed that Disney World guests would expect to see familiar rides from Disneyland when they visited the Magic Kingdom, which made the decision to shelve the new attraction proposals even easier.

As a result, Disney ultimately decided to replicate Snow White's Adventures, Peter Pan's Flight, and Mr. Toad's Wild Ride in Walt Disney World, although the Florida version of Toad did get a unique two-track layout. Today, Peter Pan's Flight is the only one of those dark rides still in operation in the Magic Kingdom.

## Finding Sleeping Beauty, Mary Poppins, Sleepy Hollow, and The Sword in the Stone Today

Unfortunately, Disney never added an attraction based on *Sleeping Beauty*, *Mary Poppins*, "The Legend of Sleepy Hollow," or *The Sword in the Stone* in the Magic Kingdom. However, fans can still find remnants from those stories in Walt Disney World today if they are willing to look hard enough. For example, the star of *Sleeping Beauty*, Aurora, can be found throughout the parks in a variety of character meet-and-greet locations, character meals, and parades. In addition, Aurora's dress is displayed behind the cash register in the Castle Couture shop in Fantasyland. Like Aurora's dress in the film, it magically changes colors to the amazement of princesses of all ages.

Although *Mary Poppins* did not get a stand-alone attraction, the film is featured as a scene in the Great Movie Ride in Disney's Hollywood Studios, with audio-animatronic versions of Mary Poppins and Bert singing on the rooftops in London. Two additional *Mary Poppins* tributes can be found just outside the Great Movie Ride. First, a beautiful window display in the Great Movie Ride façade features a tribute to *Mary Poppins*, with banners giving information about the creation of the film, and actual tickets from the movie's premiere displayed on a table. In the nearby courtyard, guests can also see the handprints and footprints of none other than Dick Van Dyke who famously played the role of Bert. Guests can also meet Mary Poppins in various locations throughout Disney World, including in the United Kingdom Pavilion in Epcot's World Showcase. A lesser-known tribute to the film is in the lobby of the Villas at the Grand Floridian, where the penguins from *Mary Poppins* can be found playing in a gorgeous fountain.

Strangely enough, the impact of "The Legend of Sleepy Hollow" on Disney World today is perhaps even stronger than the Disney films *Sleeping Beauty* and *Mary Poppins*. For example, Imagineers drew architectural inspiration from "Sleepy Hollow" and the stately manor houses of that era and geographic location when developing plans for Disney World's version of the Haunted Mansion, a dramatic Dutch-Gothic style manor house.

Sleepy Hollow Refreshments, a counter service restaurant located in Liberty Square, is a direct reference to Irving's work, and the building's architecture is based on his home (known as Sunnyside) near Tarrytown, New York.

Directly across the street from Sleepy Hollow Refreshments is the Ye Olde Christmas Shoppe, a gift shop offering a wide selection of Christmas ornaments and other holiday gifts. A sign hanging from the shop façade pays tribute to one of the stars of "The Legend of Sleepy Hollow" and reads: "Music and Voice Lessons, by appointment, Ichabod Crane Instructor."

Perhaps the greatest tribute to "Sleepy Hollow" is featured in Mickey's Not-So-Scary Halloween Party, a hard-ticketed event held on select nights in September and October in the Magic Kingdom. One of the most popular aspects of the Halloween Party is the Mickey's Boo-to-You Halloween Parade. The start of that parade is one of the most exciting experiences in all of Walt Disney World, an actual appearance by the Headless Horseman.

Finally, sitting directly behind Cinderella Castle and immediately in front of the Prince Charming Regal Carrousel in the heart of Fantasyland is a small tribute to *The Sword in the Stone*: an actual sword in a stone. It remains one of the better photo opportunities in the Magic Kingdom. The plaque on the stone reads: WHOSO PULLETH OUT THIS SWORD OF THIS STONE AND ANVIL IS RIGHTWISE RULER BORN OF ENGLAND. Just try walking by the sword and not giving it a pull!

CHAPTER THREE

# The Enchanted Snow Palace

*So, uh tell me. What made the Queen go all ice crazy?*

— Kristoff, *Frozen* (2013)

No one could have predicted the enormous success of Disney's animated film *Frozen* (2013). It became a cultural phenomenon, with children and adults across the world falling in love with the story and its characters. *Frozen* won Academy Awards for Best Animated Film and Best Original Song, *Let It Go*, which became an anthem for princesses of all ages. The film grossed more than $1 billion worldwide and became the highest grossing animated film of all time. Even Disney was shocked about the popularity and overwhelming success of its fifty-third animated film.

Following the amazing public and critical response to *Frozen*, Disney rushed to capitalize on its mammoth success by releasing a wide variety of merchandise based on the film and by creating new theme park lands, attractions, and experiences incorporating its characters. However, if the company had only listened to Imagineer Marc Davis decades earlier, an icy wienie would already exist in Fantasyland. Almost forty years prior to *Frozen's* release, Davis developed plans for a stunning theme park attraction based on the same fairy tale that inspired the Disney animated film. Unfortunately for Davis, Thunder Mesa was not the only monumental project he worked on that failed to get off the drawing board.

## Frozen Beginnings

For the uninitiated (which at this point is likely a very small group), *Frozen* tells the story of a troubled young princess, Elsa, struggling to come to grips with her power to turn everything she touches into ice and snow. Elsa's younger sister, Anna, sets out on a journey to find Elsa and to help her solve a myriad of "icy" problems. Along the way, fans are treated to memorable characters Kristoff, a rugged ice salesman; Sven, Kristoff's reindeer best friend; and Olaf, a hilarious snowman brought to life by Elsa's magical powers.

*Frozen* was loosely based on "The Snow Queen," a fairy tale by Hans Christian Andersen first published in 1844. At its core, "The Snow Queen" is a story about the eternal struggle between good and evil. While both *Frozen* and "The Snow Queen" share overarching themes of redemption, tribulation, and love, the specific details of the film and the fairy tale vary greatly.

## Plans for an Enchanted Snow Palace

Before his retirement in the late 1970s, Marc Davis developed plans for an attraction known as the Enchanted Snow Palace that, like *Frozen*, was based upon "The Snow Queen." The concept was originally developed for Disneyland's Fantasyland, but was later also considered for inclusion in Walt Disney World. Davis thought that an attraction with an icy façade and a cool (literally) interior where guests could get relief from the sizzling heat of California or Florida would be a welcome addition to the parks.

The Enchanted Snow Palace would have been...well...an actual snow palace. More specifically, it would have been an enormous white-and-blue show building, rising from the ground like a massive glacier in the arctic. Windows, doors, spires, and other decorative ornamentation would have been intricately weaved into the icy façade of the building.

Davis developed numerous pieces of gorgeous conceptual art for the Enchanted Snow Palace, several of which are depicted in the book *Marc Davis, Walt Disney's Renaissance Man* (2014). One such illustration depicts the exterior façade and includes numerous icy towers and several openings with what appears to be starlight glistening from within. It is no exaggeration to say that the Enchanted Snow Palace could have been the most beautiful building ever constructed by Disney Imagineers.

Inside the Snow Palace, guests would have enjoyed a boat ride that would take them on a magical journey down a river of melted ice. The striking white-and-blue colors from the exterior façade of the show building would continue to flow through the interior of the attraction. The boats would have been similar to those used in Pirates of the Caribbean and It's a Small World. *The Nutcracker Suite* by Pyotr Ilyich Tchaikovsky would serve as the background score of the attraction. Imagineers even contemplated incorporating an aurora borealis effect on the ceiling.

As depicted in Davis' numerous concept drawings, guests would have travelled past richly themed scenes of arctic landscapes complete with numerous audio-animatronic animals. One humorous illustration depicts two polar bears, one adult and one child, each standing on one foot as if they were in the middle of a frigid dance routine. Other Davis illustrations depict playful penguins and walruses, icy ballerinas, and trees covered in snow that strangely resemble human forms. The boats would eventually enter a magical snow cave with frost giants and ice fairies (almost identical to those depicted in the 1940 Disney animated film *Fantasia*) scattered about the landscape.

After passing several snowy handmaidens, guests would finally enter the domain of the star of the attraction, the Snow Queen. Perhaps the most stunning piece of artwork produced by Davis for the Enchanted Snow Palace depicts the Snow Queen in all of her icy glory. Her beautiful white-and-blue gown drifts to the ground and seems to flow into the surrounding snow and ice. She wears a dramatic crown with icy spikes jetting high above her head. The Snow Queen is surrounded by an assortment of solid white creatures, including a snowy owl and several snowshoe hares.

The attraction would culminate in a journey with the Snow Queen through a powerful blizzard before finally returning to safety. Like so many other attractions in Fantasyland, the entire family could have enjoyed the Enchanted Snow Palace together.

Although the conceptual artwork was breathtaking, the significant price tag for the attraction was equally breathtaking. At the time Davis developed these plans, Disney was shifting its focus to attractions that appealed to adults (such as Space Mountain). This emphasis was compounded by the fact that Fantasyland was already home to several "family" attractions, including Peter Pan's Flight and Mr. Toad's Wild Ride. As a result, plans for the Enchanted Snow Palace melted as Disney executives ultimately decided to focus their financial resources elsewhere.

## Finding the Snow Queen in Walt Disney World Today

Although the Enchanted Snow Palace never made it into Disney World, *Frozen* has stormed like a blizzard into the Florida parks. On June 21, 2016, Frozen Ever After opened in the space formerly occupied by Maelstrom in the Norway Pavilion at Epcot's World Showcase. This re-themed indoor boat ride allows guests to "Hoist the sails in Arendelle aboard an ancient Norwegian vessel" as guests sail through the "wintery world of *Frozen*." Guests can also visit the Royal Sommerhus at the Norway Pavilion, the summer getaway for Anna, Elsa, and all of their friends. The *Frozen* characters and a wide variety of merchandise from the film can also be seen in many other locations throughout Walt Disney World. With a *Frozen* sequel already announced, the significant impact of this film franchise on Walt Disney World will surely continue for the foreseeable future.

While these additions create a great deal of excitement in the parks, as a fan of Disney history, it is difficult for me to walk through Fantasyland and not imagine how beautiful the Enchanted Snow Palace might have been. However, the best piece of advice that I can give anyone longing for the Davis' Snow Palace is to...let it go!

## CHAPTER FOUR

# Fire Mountain and Villains Mountain

*Walt Disney always felt that the most significant thing about the past was the experience and preparation it gave his Company for the future; and in that spirit, we are moving forward aggressively with new projects designed to expand our capacity and ability to provide our family audience with the finest in recreation and entertainment.*

— 1972 Annual Report, Walt Disney Productions

The Disney "mountain range" is a moniker given to a collection of popular attractions themed as mountains. The range consists of Space Mountain, Big Thunder Mountain Railroad, Splash Mountain, and the Seven Dwarfs Mine Train in the Magic Kingdom, and Expedition Everest in the Animal Kingdom.

Each Disney mountain is an "E-ticket" attraction, an old Disney label for the most popular attractions in the parks. They are visual landmarks that grab the attention of theme park guests and pull them to Tomorrowland, Frontierland, Fantasyland, and Asia, respectively. More than other attractions, the Disney mountains build enormous anticipation and excitement for park guests and cause them to arrive early and sprint to the mountains as soon as the gates open. That is how the phrases "dash to Splash" and "race to Space" came to be.

Following the closure of one of the Magic Kingdom's most popular attractions in 1994, Disney Imagineers began developing plans for not one, but two additional breathtaking mountains to serve as possible replacements. One option was Fire Mountain, a unique roller-coaster attraction set within a volcano straight out of a Jules Verne novel. The second was Villains Mountain, a log flume attraction paying homage to Maleficent, Ursula, Captain Hook, and other Disney villains. What is even more exciting is that, at one point, Disney executives seriously considered adding *both* mountains to the Magic Kingdom! Why was neither mountain ever constructed? The answer to that question begins with the controversial closure of another Fantasyland favorite, 20,000 Leagues Under the Sea: Submarine Voyage.

## 20,000 Leagues Under the Sea Submarine Voyage

Since the day that it first opened in the Magic Kingdom on October 14, 1971, 20,000 Leagues Under the Sea was an immediate fan-favorite attraction. Based on the classic 1954 Disney live-action film of the same name starring James Mason as the mysterious Captain Nemo and Kirk Douglas as the confident harpooner Ned Land, the 20,000 Leagues attraction offered guests the opportunity to board actual submarines and go on a captivating underwater adventure. In *Walt Disney World, The First Decade* (1982), the attraction was described as follows:

> Submarines styled after the *Nautilus* sail from a peaceful tropical lagoon on a journey through coral reefs to a vast sunless cavern, descending into an ocean of untold mysteries.

Set behind the majestic towers of Cinderella Castle, 20,000 Leagues Under the Sea occupied an enormous footprint in Fantasyland covering approximately one-quarter of it, including a man-made lagoon that held over eleven million gallons of water.

The attraction featured perhaps the most visually stunning ride vehicles ever created for a Disney attraction in the form of large submarines that would hold approximately forty passengers each. The submarines themselves were a sight to behold. With a distinct patina green color and a unique design, the vessels looked as though they had been pulled directly from the pages of Jules Verne's classic novel. The fleet consisted of twelve submarines, with a thirteenth buried in the lagoon itself for visual effect.

Despite its popularity, 20,000 Leagues Under the Sea closed in September 1994. Disney characterized the closure as temporary before admitting in 1996 that the attraction was indeed closed for good. Why was the attraction closed when it was still popular with park guests? Extremely high maintenance costs, lack of handicap accessibility, and frustration of cast members responsible for painstakingly maintaining the attraction are all rumored to have been contributing factors.

Even though 20,000 Leagues Under the Sea occupied a valuable piece of real estate in Fantasyland, the area remained mostly dormant in the years that followed its closure. In the late 1990s, Disney Imagineers began weighing numerous options for replacing 20,000 Leagues Under the Sea. At this time, public demand for "thrill" attractions in amusement parks was rising and Disney knew it had to meet this demand in the Magic Kingdom. With that in mind, the Imagineers considered two primary replacement options: Fire Mountain and Villains Mountain.

## Fire Mountain

The Imagineers who worked on the Fire Mountain concept wanted to stay loyal to the Jules Verne theming reflected in 20,000 Leagues Under the Sea. They developed plans for an innovative roller-coaster thrill attraction set inside a massive show building that would be themed as a smoking volcano. The volcano itself would have been enormous and dramatic, dominating the skyline of Fantasyland behind Cinderella Castle.

While a roller coaster set within another "mountain" may sound simple and repetitive given the mountains that already existed in the Magic Kingdom (Space, Splash, and Big Thunder), the Fire Mountain ride experience would have been revolutionary. The attraction would start just as many other attractions in Disney World did, with guests boarding ride vehicles with the track that actually moved the vehicles lying underneath. However, halfway through the attraction when the volcano was just about to erupt, Fire Mountain would transform into a "flying" coaster, with the coaster track now above guests' heads while glowing hot lava from the volcano's eruption poured beneath them. After escaping the mountain's fiery fury, the attraction would return to its initial form prior to the end of the attraction, with the coaster track again below the ride vehicles.

In order for the Fire Mountain concept to be viable, Disney needed an intellectual property franchise to associate with it. Imagineers found what they believed to be the perfect movie tie-in when they discovered that the Disney studio was developing an animated film that had submarines, adventurers, exotic locations, and most importantly, a large volcano: *Atlantis: The Lost Empire.*

*Atlantis* was released in 2001, and was created using traditional animation techniques at a time when computer-generated animation was taking the industry by storm. The film tells the story of a young linguist and cartographer, Milo James Thatch, who finds a sacred book that turns out to be a map to the lost city of Atlantis. The film starred Michael J. Fox as Thatch, with James Garner, Jim Varney, and Leonard Nimoy lending voice talents for other characters.

Rumors about the addition of Fire Mountain were rampant in the late 1990s. In 1998, the *Orlando Business Journal* published an article about the increased prevalence of thrill rides in Disney World entitled "Guests Get Their Thrills from Local Theme Parks." In regard to Fire Mountain, it stated:

> Speculation is circulating about the next mountain at the Magic Kingdom—Fire Mountain. It would replace 20,000 Leagues Under the Sea, which closed several years ago, and would feature a theme based on an upcoming Disney movie, *Atlantis*.
>
> Guests would feel like they were flying through the roller coaster as they make their way through Lava Lake and through the mountain. For the flying experience, guests would lie down facing the ground and would be suspended throughout the ride.

As Disney executives weighed the feasibility of Fire Mountain, some worried that an attraction themed as a volcano would be out of place in Fantasyland. Balancing this concern with the true excitement of the executives about the project, the Imagineers eventually decided that Fire Mountain would be a better fit thematically in Adventureland. They considered adding Fire Mountain between Pirates of the Caribbean in Adventureland and Splash Mountain in Frontierland or, alternatively, between Pirates and the Jungle Cruise. The mountain itself would have been visible from all corners of Adventureland and, perhaps most visually stunning, from the Polynesian Resort on the shores of the Seven Seas Lagoon.

While the Fire Mountain attraction would have been revolutionary, the hefty price tag associated with developing an intricately themed mountain and new innovative ride technology was a large hurdle to overcome. Because of these concerns, the conceptual plans for Fire Mountain morphed into a simpler flying coaster with no "switch" incorporated in the ride system

## Villains Mountain

While one group of Imagineers was hard at work on Fire Mountain, a different group worked to develop plans for another stunning Mountain attraction, this one devoted to the realm of Disney villains. A villain's concept may seem like a strange addition to the fairytale theming of Fantasyland, but Disney executives were well aware that villains were extremely popular with theme park guests. Toys, shirts, and other merchandise featuring Maleficent, Captain Hook, Jafar, and other Disney villains were flying off the shelves, and the executives believed that customer demand existed for a villains-based attraction.

The attraction's exterior would have drawn inspiration from "Night on Bald Mountain," a segment in the 1940 Disney animated film *Fantasia*. In this segment, the sinister demon Chernabog calls upon an ominous variety of ghosts, skeletons, spirits, and other demons to join an evil ceremony. The spooky spirits dance as Chernabog orchestrates from high above the rocky peaks of Bald Mountain. This ghostly gathering only ends when church bells ring and a choir begins to sing in the town at the base of the mountain. Due to this inspiration, Imagineers even considered calling the attraction Bald Mountain.

Villains Mountain would have been a log-flume experience reminiscent of Splash Mountain. Instead of focusing on one or two villains, the attraction would be themed as a salute to all Disney villains, who had gathered deep in the mountain in an effort to take over the Magic Kingdom.

Guests would board boats similar to Splash Mountain, Pirates of the Caribbean, and It's a Small World and float through a series of tableaus featuring a variety of Disney villains. At the climax, they would come face to face with the signature villain from *Sleeping Beauty*, the evil fairy Maleficent, before falling down a steep, adrenaline-pumping plunge to the base of the mountain.

Imagineers anticipated that Villains Mountain would occupy a similar footprint in Fantasyland as its predecessor, 20,000 Leagues Under the Sea. However, plans for the concept continued to morph and evolve. At one point, Disney even considered adding a Villains Village, an entirely new sub-area in Fantasyland devoted to the bad guys and girls from Disney animated films. It would have included numerous shops and villain character encounters set along a cobblestone street, with Villains Mountain looming ominously in the background as the area's marquee centerpiece.

## Which Mountain?

Disney executives and Imagineers were excited about the potential of both Fire Mountain and Villains Mountain. Choosing between them would be difficult. As such, Disney management made the smartest decision they could: they punted to the chairman and CEO of the Disney company, Michael Eisner. To Eisner's credit, he recognized the brilliance of both ideas. In fact, he liked Fire Mountain and Villains Mountain so much that he wanted to add both attractions to the Magic Kingdom!

Disney executives felt so strongly about the villain concept that they considered, in lieu of an entirely separate land in the Magic Kingdom, developing a standalone theme park dedicated to Disney villains. As a result, they did not want to place a marque villains attraction in the Magic Kingdom when it could be best used in a separate park. The Villains Mountain concept was therefore temporarily shelved until the company could decide exactly what it wanted to do. Unfortunately, to this point, Disney has not moved forward with a standalone villains theme park or land. Therefore, the Villains Mountain concept remains on the shelves at Walt Disney Imagineering waiting for its time to come, assuming it ever does.

Imagineers also planned on moving forward with Fire Mountain in Adventureland, but the momentum for that addition also slowed and was eventually shelved altogether. While we don't know for sure why that occurred, the significant expense required to construct the attraction combined with the disappointment of *Atlantis* at the box office no doubt played a large part in Fire Mountain's demise. *Atlantis* grossed over $180 million worldwide, but Disney still considered that number a disappointment given the large budget for the film and Disney's high pre-release expectations. A 2001 *USA Today* article by Susan Wloszczyna entitled "Toons Get Their Very Own Oscar Category" elaborated on the company's disappointment:

> Animation head Thomas Schumacher says that no one could have predicted six years ago when *Atlantis* was first discussed that audiences would take a pass on a no-song action epic whose style is based on a rugged graphic novel. "It seemed like a good idea at the time to not do a sweet fairy tale," he says. "But we missed."

## An Even Grander Addition

The site of the 20,000 Leagues Under the Sea attraction, including its massive lagoon, remained relatively untouched for a decade after the attraction closed. In 2004, the lagoon was finally drained and filled. Pooh's Playful Spot, a playground for children themed to Winnie the Pooh and his friends from Hundred Acre Wood, opened in this area in 2005.

Disney did eventually move forward with a monumental project in this section of the park when it announced a massive expansion of Fantasyland in 2009. It was the largest expansion ever for the Magic Kingdom, more than doubling the size of the existing Fantasyland and providing for the addition of two new themed areas: the Enchanted Forest and Storybook Circus.

The Fantasyland addition also brought with it a long overdue new Disney Mountain when the Seven Dwarfs Mine Train opened to the public in May 2014. Although no volcano was included to pay tribute to the Fire Mountain concept, guests do get to see one Disney villain in the form of the Evil Queen from *Snow White* at the very end of the attraction.

For those sentimentalists who, like me, long for the days when 20,000 Leagues Under the Sea delighted guests with exciting underwater adventures, numerous tributes to the attraction can be found throughout Fantasyland. Inside Mr. Sanderz tree in the queue for the Many Adventures of Winnie the Pooh, directly above the door, a small *Nautilus* submarine is carved into the wood. A second Nautilus impression is included in the queue for Under the Sea ~ Journey of the Little Mermaid in New Fantasyland. Another hidden tribute to 20,000 Leagues Under the Sea can be found high atop the adjacent Cartographer's Shop; that building's weather vane is in the shape of a squid. For a nostalgic Walt Disney World fan like me, these tributes always put a smile on my face.

CHAPTER FIVE

# *Alien* Attractions

*Final report of the commercial starship* Nostromo, *third officer reporting. The other members of the crew—Kane, Lambert, Parker, Brett, Ash, and Captain Dallas—are dead. Cargo and ship destroyed. I should reach the frontier in about six weeks. With a little luck, the network will pick me up. This is Ripley, last survivor of the Nostromo, signing off.*

— Ripley, *Alien* (1979)

The Magic Kingdom is a place of fanciful delight where people of all ages and from all walks of life can come together and have fun in a family-friendly environment. Guests can walk down the perfect small town street toward a picturesque storybook castle, ride on rocket ships in a future that never was, sail on pirate ships, ride in tea cups in the middle of a castle courtyard, and cling to magic carpets on a journey around an Arabian marketplace. In short, the Magic Kingdom, perhaps more than any other place on Earth, is the epitome of family entertainment. Because of the painstaking effort taken by Imagineers to craft and maintain this wholesome family ideal, they would never consider adding an attraction based on a terrifying R-rated film... right? Unbelievably, Imagineers did just that when they contemplated adding multiple attraction concepts based on the 1979 science fiction film *Alien*.

## A New Era

The year 1984 marked the beginning of a new era for The Walt Disney Company when Michael Eisner was named its chairman and CEO. Although many now view Eisner's legacy in a negative light, no one can deny that he took the reins at Disney with an unbridled enthusiasm to make changes and move the company in a new direction.

One of Eisner's initial focuses was to increase attendance at the Disney theme parks. This emphasis reportedly arose when Eisner asked his teenage son Breck to join him on a trip to Disneyland. Breck declined the offer because Disneyland was "lame." At that point, Eisner was convinced that he had to make the theme parks more attractive for the entire family, not just children.

Eisner tasked Imagineers with developing new theme park ideas that would appeal to an older age group. As a result, Disney developed attractions such as Star Tours, a motion-based simulator attraction based on George Lucas' popular *Star Wars* franchise, and Captain EO, a 3D film directed by Francis Ford Coppola and starring Michael Jackson and Anjelica Houston.

As crazy as it may seem today, a group of Imagineers next considered an even more radical concept: adding an attraction based on a science fiction/horror film with a gruesome, terrifying alien as its marquee character. Even better, Imagineers wanted to include this attraction in the most family-friendly place on Earth: the Magic Kingdom.

## *Alien*

*Alien* was released in 1979 and became an overwhelming commercial and critical success. It is still considered a groundbreaking film in both the science fiction and horror genres. *Alien* tells the story of the crew of a commercial spacecraft known as the USCSS *Nostromo*. While returning home, the crew of the *Nostromo* encounter a vicious, predatory alien that terrorizes all aboard the ship.

*Alien* was directed by Ridley Scott and starred a young Sigourney Weaver in the role of Ripley. Far from a Disney classic, *Alien* was rated R by the Motion Picture Association of America and depicted a dirty, gritty vision of the future. The film won an Academy Award for Best Visual Effects and spawned numerous sequel, prequel, and spinoff films.

Acting on the emphasis to incorporate more experiences that appealed to teens and adults, a group of Imagineers began working on plans for an attraction based on *Alien*. They felt that such an attraction would attract teenage visitors to the park and provide a needed boost to Tomorrowland and the Magic Kingdom as a whole. Any proposed concept based on *Alien* was significant in that it would have been the first Magic Kingdom attraction themed around an R-rated film.

## Nostromo

The first iteration of a proposed *Alien* attraction was a dark ride called Nostromo, a reference to the spacecraft featured in the film. Guests would have ventured deep into space as part of a rescue mission, entering the vessel *Nostromo* to find the missing members of its crew. Travelling through the dark industrial corridors of the ship, guests would use laser cannons to protect themselves against any trouble they might encounter. They would eventually meet the frightening signature creature from *Alien*.

Not surprisingly, some Imagineers were appalled by the possibility of incorporating an *Alien*-based attraction in Disney World. To them, *Alien* contradicted everything that the Magic Kingdom and Tomorrowland represented. Instead of a clean, bright, happy vision of the future, *Alien* represented a dirty, grimy, depressing future. Instead of inspiring happiness, laughter, and glee with park guests, Nostromo would have caused fear and terror. Instead of sending guests home with a smile on their face, Nostromo would have sent them home with tears in their eyes.

Ultimately, the Nostromo attraction was abandoned. The anti-*Alien* Imagineers convinced Disney executives, including Eisner, that an attraction based on an R-rated film that would have frightened both children and adults alike and was not a good fit for the family-focused Tomorrowland. As such, the Nostromo plans were shelved. However, despite this roadblock, a group of Imagineers refused to give up on an *Alien* attraction concept.

## Yesterdayland

When the Magic Kingdom first opened on October 1, 1971, Tomorrowland was supposed to provide a realistic look into the future. It was rooted in real-world scientific advancement and achievement. However, Imagineers soon discovered that maintaining a plausible vision of the future was difficult. The problem with tomorrow is that it quickly becomes today. Maintaining this portrayal of Tomorrowland would require frequent updates and upkeep, which did not happen in the decades that followed.

As an example of this conundrum, the early version of Tomorrowland included an attraction called Flight to the Moon that opened on December 24, 1971. In this attraction, guests sat in a circular theatre for a simulated journey to the moon with the help of flight director Mr. Tom Morrow. The preshow of the attraction stated that the experience was taking place "sometime" in the future. The problem was that an actual flight to the moon had already happened in 1969, two years before Flight to the Moon's opening. Therefore, it did not exactly represent a "futuristic" concept. The attraction was changed in 1975 to Mission to Mars, which provided a similar journey, this time to the Red Planet.

Over the course of the next fifteen years, Tomorrowland remained largely unchanged and quickly grew outdated. Some Imagineers joked that Tomorrowland should be renamed to Yesterdayland.

In the early 1990s, Disney executives considered a massive overhaul of Tomorrowland's theming. In dealing with the Yesterdayland problem, the Imagineers developed a plan for a new Tomorrowland that would be the future as seen through the eyes of individuals from the 1950s and 1960s. New Tomorrowland would be a science-fictional future in the mold of Jules Verne, H.G. Wells, and Buck Rodgers. It would be an actual working city where people and aliens all lived, worked, and played together. Best of all, it would be a future that would never be out of date.

In the Disney company's 1993 Annual Report, Disney stated:

> Imagineers are working on a whole new Tomorrowland that will take shape in the next three years. There they will create the look of a 'lived in" Future City.

New Tomorrowland would be the future that never was and always would be.

## Alien Encounter

The Mission to Mars attraction had grown stale with park guests and, as part of the Tomorrowland renovation, Imagineers felt that a new attraction was needed. Accordingly, Imagineers again considered incorporating an *Alien*-based attraction, this time set within the circular theatre that had previously housed Flight to the Moon and Mission to Mars.

The new attraction would be called Alien Encounter, and would feature the titular creature from *Alien* who would eventually be released in the theatre's interior. Notably, the attraction would have taken place completely in the dark, with a variety of special effects including heat, water, and wind convincing guests that the creature was behind them, above them, breathing down their necks, and even drooling on their shoulders.

What made Alien Encounter so attractive to Disney executives was that, due to using many of the existing features of the Mission to Mars theatre and the relatively simple effects needed to create the experience, it would have been cheap to construct. Eisner loved the idea and gave Imagineers the go-ahead to begin production.

As was the case with the Nostromo concept, certain Disney Imagineers remained shocked that Disney would green light a terrifying attraction based on an R-rated film. The concerned Imagineers brought their complaints to Eisner. However, the benefits of the proposed Alien Encounter attraction were too strong for him to ignore. First, Alien Encounter would meet Eisner's goal of providing an attraction that would entertain teens and adults. Since *Alien* was such a popular film, guests would immediately recognize the name, which would self-market the attraction without Disney having to do anything. It would also remove the need for Imagineers to spend time and expense creating a backstory.

The anti-*Alien* Imagineers didn't give up. They took their case to someone they thought Eisner would listen to...George Lucas! Imagineers supposedly made their case to Lucas that Alien Encounter was too intense for children and did not fit in Tomorrowland or anywhere else in the Magic Kingdom. Lucas was deeply involved with the Disney company at this time. He had consulted on the Star Tours project for Disney's Hollywood Studios (at the time known as the Disney-MGM Studios) and was in the middle of developing the Indiana Jones Adventure for Disneyland. As the story goes, Lucas agreed with these Imagineers and committed to talk with Eisner.

Eisner soon called a meeting with the Alien Encounter Imagineering team and told them he had changed his mind about the project. He now felt that the Alien Encounter proposal, and in particular the signature creature from *Alien*, was too intense for the Magic Kingdom. However, he did not scrap the project altogether. Instead, he tasked Imagineers with developing their own alien, one that would hopefully be a little less frightening and intimidating for theme park guests.

## ExtraTERRORestrial Alien Encounter

Imagineers went back to the drawing board and developed plans for the ExtraTERRORestrial Alien Encounter. This version of Alien Encounter officially opened in 1995 (although soft openings took place in December of 1994) and also featured an alien creature released in the old Mission to Mars theatre with a variety of effects used to frighten guests.

Because they could not rely on the *Alien* backstory, Imagineers developed a new one centered on a fictional company known as X-S Tech, a futuristic technology company. X-S Tech would provide a marketing pitch to theme park guests advertising their teleportation services that were described as being "practically painless." Not surprisingly, this presentation would go drastically wrong, and an alien creature would soon be released into the audience.

ExtraTERRORrestrial Alien Encounter was scarier than anything else in the Magic Kingdom up to that time (hence the all caps TERROR in the name). Disney described it as "quite possibly the most frightening attraction ever created." Some guests found it downright terrifying. For a variety of reasons, including the scare factor, Alien Encounter closed in October of 2003 after an eight-year run in Tomorrowland.

The attraction remains hotly debated in Walt Disney World circles today. Some feel that it was a much-needed adult attraction that brilliantly combined a variety of special effects to simulate an actual alien encounter. Others feel that it was an absolute abomination that should have never been included in the Magic Kingdom in the first place. Either way, ExtraTERRORrestrial exemplifies how some ideas never quite go away at Disney.

## Finding Aliens in Walt Disney World Today

Tomorrowland did finally get an attraction where guests could use laser cannons to shoot aliens when Buzz Lightyear Space Ranger Spin opened in 1998. However, the fun and upbeat *Toy Story*-based attraction is a far cry from the original Nostromo concept.

In 2004, Stitch's Great Escape opened in the former Mission to Mars/ Alien Encounter theatre, and has been entertaining or disappointing guests (depending on your preferences) ever since. Based on the 2002 Disney film *Lilo and Stitch*, the attraction follows the familiar pattern of an alien escaping into the circular theatre and providing numerous frights for park guests. However, the difference today is that these scares are much more light-hearted and comical in nature. Instead of worrying about getting eaten by an alien, the biggest concern for guests now is dealing with a burped chili dog smell, thanks to Stitch. Disney recently announced that Stitch's Great Escape was going to a "seasonal" opening schedule, meaning that the attraction will only be open during busier times of the year. This is usually the "beginning of the end" for park attractions, and so in the near future Stitch's space could once again be re-themed.

Although a standalone *Alien* attraction never came to be in Disney World, *Alien* and its signature monster did find a home in the Great Movie Ride at Disney's Hollywood Studios. In that attraction, guests enter a scene dedicated to *Alien*, where they travel through the dingy interior of the *Nostromo* before being confronted by the frightening creature from the film.

PART TWO

# EPCOT

*But the most exciting and by far the most important part of our Florida project—in fact, the heart of everything we'll be doing in Disney World—will be our Experimental Prototype [Community] of Tomorrow. We call it EPCOT."*

— Walt Disney

CHAPTER SIX

# Experimental Prototype Community of Tomorrow

*The tiniest spark of an idea is no small thing. Even if born upon the tattered edge of a paper napkin, it may very well grow up to be the size of something special.*

—The Imagineers, *Walt Disney Imagineering, A Behind the Dreams Look at Making the Magic Real* (1996)

While the plans for all of Walt Disney World's four major theme parks morphed and evolved from what Disney executives and Imagineers originally contemplated to what eventually opened to guests, none come close to Epcot in terms of how drastic the scope of those changes turned out to be. In fact, the Epcot that guests experienced on the park's opening day, October 1, 1982, had *almost* nothing in common with the "city of tomorrow" that Walt Disney himself dreamed of in the 1960s.

Initial plans for Epcot contemplated an actual working city, a utopian city, where people from different walks of life would live, work, and play together in a clean, efficient, innovative, and aesthetically pleasing environment. Epcot would have displayed the latest in technological advancement and the "ingenuity and imagination of American free enterprise." It would have worked to solve the problems of urban blight faced by cities around the world, and would have served as a beacon of inspiration for urban leaders to improve their own cities.

So how did Epcot change from an actual working city to the "permanent world's fair" that eventually opened in 1982? The answer to that question begins with the grand aspirations and dreams of Walt Disney himself for the Florida Project as a whole, and the unfortunate struggles and practical dilemmas faced by the Disney company following Walt's death in 1966.

## The 1965 Press Conference

In 1965, mysterious companies began purchasing thousands of acres of land in central Florida near the sleepy town of Orlando. These purchasers included oddly named entities like Reedy Creek Ranch Corporation, Latin-American Development and Management Corporation, and Tomahawk Properties, Incorporated. When completed, these large-scale land acquisitions totaled approximately twenty-seven thousand acres at a collective purchase price of more than $5 million.

Not surprisingly, wild rumors swirled about the true identity of the purchaser behind these strange corporate veils. In *Since the World Began, Walt Disney World The First 25 Years* (1996), author Jeff Kurtti described this wide-ranging speculation:

> Because of the proximity of the properties to Cape Canaveral and the Kennedy Space Center, aerospace industrial firms were believed likely buyers. McDonnell Aircraft, Republic Aviation, Douglas Aviation, and Lockheed were discussed in the press. Hercules Powder Company, Ford, Volkswagen, Chrysler, and Philco were all mentioned. David Rockefeller and Howard Hughes were considered possible buyers. And Disney still popped up every now and then.

The *Orlando Sentinel* ran an article on October 17, 1965, proclaiming that Walt Disney was the secret buyer. After weeks of speculation (and despite Florida Governor Hayden Burns confirming the rumor a few weeks earlier), an official press conference was held on November 15, 1965, at Orlando's Cherry Plaza Hotel. Walt Disney, his brother Roy, and Governor Burns gathered to formally announce to the public that Disney was indeed the mystery purchaser of approximately forty-three square miles of swampland in central Florida.

Walt said that, as part of his Florida Project, another Disneyland-style theme park would be constructed. For the first time in a public forum, he also stated his grand intentions of building a "city of tomorrow." Although from today's perspective the Magic Kingdom is the most popular theme park in the world, many believe that Walt's dream of Epcot was the driving force behind the Florida land acquisitions and the Florida Project as a whole.

Over the course of the next year, Disney executives and Imagineers worked in a frenzy to advance "Phase One" of the Florida Project, most notably developing plans for the Magic Kingdom theme park that would serve as the initial economic driving force for the entire development. However, Walt also tasked a separate group of Imagineers with developing plans for his Experimental Prototype Community of Tomorrow.

## Initial Plans for the Florida Project

Walt's initial plans for Disney World did not include four separate theme parks, two water parks, two miniature golf courses, and the numerous other offerings that guests enjoy today. How do we know that? Simple. Walt himself told the world in surprising detail what he planned to do in Florida.

Walt's initial conceptual plans for the Florida Project were depicted on a famous 1966 sketch that became known as Disney's Seventh Preliminary Master Plot Plan. The sketch is captivating in that it is very rough, but immensely detailed, and depicts a series of specified areas running from south to north on the newly acquired Disney property, all of which would be connected by a futuristic monorail transportation system.

A "perfect" city would certainly need access to an airport, and Epcot was no exception. The airport would sit at the southern end of the Disney property, and would rely on cutting-edge technology to more efficiently transport both passengers and their baggage. Just north of the airport would be an entrance complex for the entire Disney property and an industrial park that would be home to numerous corporations that would work on, test, and implement a variety of advanced technologies. At the far northern edge of the Disney property would be the Magic Kingdom. In the middle of the development, and at the heart of the entire Florida Project, was Epcot.

Walt's passion for Epcot was unbridled. In developing ideas and concepts for Epcot, he reached out to and drew inspiration from a multitude of industry leaders across the country. In *Realityland, True-Life Adventures at Walt Disney World* (2007), author David Koenig detailed this effort:

> Walt had letters of inquiry sent to 500 corporations seeking their participation. The goal was not just to sell, but to learn. Walt himself visited a few of the larger companies, but sent Joe Potter to tour 100 different factories, research laboratories, and think tanks, among them Westinghouse, General Electric, Bell, IBM, RCA, and Rockwell International.

## The Epcot Film

"Welcome to a little bit of Florida here in California." Those are the words Walt Disney spoke on October 27, 1966, to begin the famous "Epcot film," a twenty-five minute piece of Disney nostalgia that provided an overview of the entire Florida Project. For many, the very thought of Walt Disney immediately conjures images of this classic piece of Disney history.

The film was played on February 2, 1967 (a few months after Walt's death) to a group of Florida business executives and political leaders. It served as part marketing pitch and part educational presentation on the

Florida Project, with primary emphasis placed on Epcot. This initial screening was even more important given the significant legislative package that Disney would later seek to, among other things, create the Reedy Creek Improvement District that would give the Disney company a great deal of autonomy and discretion for development and construction of the property.

Imagineer Marty Sklar penned the legendary narration of the film, which Walt recited in captivating fashion. The film was recorded in a large studio meticulously decorated to appear as "The Florida Conference Room at WED Enterprises' Glendale headquarters." The room was filled floor to ceiling with numerous conceptual renderings, schematics, and models that, even without the narration, were impressive enough to capture the imagination of viewers of all ages.

In his book *Dream It! Do It!* (2013), Sklar recounts a meeting he had with Walt Disney about the concept of Epcot, and provides the following seven "key points" he jotted down during that meeting, from which Sklar developed Walt's monologue for the Epcot film:

- EPCOT will be a showcase to the world of American free enterprise.
- In EPCOT, we can show what could be done with proper city planning.
- The philosophy behind EPCOT is the same as Disneyland: people will be king.
- EPCOT's starting point: the needs of people (transportation, education, etc.).
- Hit all the problems—tick them off—because if we control, we won't let them get to be problems.
- EPCOT will be a working community. People who grow up here will have skills in pace with the needs of today's world.
- Disneyland: a few years ago, it was "far out"...a dream...nobody believed [in] it. But it had a philosophy founded in a belief in people, and it answered their needs. We have the experience to do EPCOT based on our practical experience in Disneyland.

Director Ham Luske and Art Director Mac Stewart took Sklar's outline and developed a conceptual storyboard for Epcot's layout. These initial plans called for a cutting-edge metropolitan area that would have addressed many of the problems faced by urban environments during that time.

For his own part, Walt described his inspiration for Epcot as follows:

> I don't believe there's a challenge anywhere in the world that's more important to people everywhere than finding solutions to the problems of our cities. But where do we begin; how do we start answering this great challenge?

> Well, we're convinced we must start with the public need. And the need is not just for curing the old ills of old cities. We think the need is for starting from scratch on virgin land and building a special kind of new community.
>
> We don't presume to know all the answers. In fact, we're counting on the cooperation of American industry to provide their best thinking during the planning and creation of our Experimental Prototype Community of Tomorrow.
>
> So that's what Epcot is: an experimental prototype community that will always be in a state of becoming. It will never cease to be a living blueprint of the future...."

In the Epcot film, an exceedingly upbeat and energetic Walt made clear that Epcot was indeed the "heart" of the Florida Project. Walt's passion for the entire Florida Project generally and Epcot specifically jumped off the screen and was impossible to ignore.

## The Epcot Layout

Part of what made the Epcot film so captivating is the amazing level of detail Walt provided about the Florida Project. Epcot would utilize a "radial plan" whereby a network of transportation spokes would radiate from a central urban hub. This was similar to the hub-and-spoke layout used in the conceptual design of Disneyland, but provided for concentric circles that radiated out from the hub, with each circle designated for certain specific uses.

Based on the Epcot film, as well as a series of gorgeous conceptual drawings by Disney artist Herb Ryman, we know that the initial plans for Epcot specified a layout of four concentric spheres. The innermost sphere would serve as Epcot's business and commercial center. Included in this sphere was the marquee centerpiece for Epcot, a thirty-story cosmopolitan hotel towering above the development like a beacon of the future. Among other offerings, the hotel would have featured a seven-acre pedestrian deck standing high above the main-level foot traffic, with a series of trees and water elements incorporated therein to create a peaceful, pedestrian friendly environment. It would also feature a world-class spa and numerous other guest entertainment options. The area surrounding the hotel would include a wide variety of office buildings, theatres, restaurants, and other entertainment options with an international theme spread across approximately fifty acres (no doubt a thematic predecessor to Epcot's World Showcase).

The next ring closest to the urban center would be high-density, multi-family (apartment) housing that would have provided residential living options for individuals working in the city.

The third ring from the center would consist of a broad "greenbelt" area featuring numerous social and recreation options including parks, schools, churches, and playgrounds. This would be the "rural" component of the otherwise futuristic city with trees, bushes, and other "green" landscaping features incorporated therein.

The outermost ring would have consisted of low-density, single-family residential housing options that would serve as the suburban center for Epcot. One interesting aspect of this suburban area is that it would be purely residential, with no mixture of commercial buildings or businesses that might negatively impact the visual integrity of the area. In other words, residents would not have been able to go next door to the grocery store to buy a loaf of bread or a gallon of milk.

Transportation would have played an integral part in Epcot and would have focused on efficiency, safety, and minimal environmental impact. Although the Epcot film declares that pedestrian traffic would be king, a variety of other transportation options would be available to residents and guests.

Directly below the hotel in the commercial hub of Epcot would be a massive, multi-level transportation lobby from which two separate electrical transportation systems would travel in and out. For long-distance travel, a series of monorails would take guests from Epcot to and from the adjacent Magic Kingdom theme park and a proposed one thousand acre industrial park.

For shorter distance commutes, WEDWay PeopleMover trams would transport commuters to and from the urban center, residential living areas, and the green belt. The WEDWay vehicles would travel via motors that were completely separate from the trams and embedded in the tracks. The WEDWay trams would continuously run, resulting in no traffic lights or corresponding traffic jams. By focusing on these modes of transportation, Epcot could eliminate pollution, traffic problems, and unsightly parking lots and parking decks.

Traditional automobiles, trucks, and buses would be allowed in Epcot, but only through specified routes. As clarified in the Epcot film, transportation would take place on three separate levels of the transportation lobby. On the bottom level, truck transportation would be used to deliver commercial supplies to local businesses. A middle level would be reserved for automobile transportation and for hotel and apartment parking. The top level of transportation would be the above-referenced monorail and WEDWay trams that would radiate from the transportation lobby to the high-density apartment housing, the recreational areas, and the single-family suburban residential areas.

Perhaps the most amazing part of the Epcot conceptual plans, and probably the most unrealistic, was that the innermost sphere (the urban center) would have been completely enclosed in a dome. This would have allowed for a climate-controlled environment that would ensure ideal weather year-round. While this concept was certainly not practical, it is still fascinating to imagine.

In terms of capacity, Walt anticipated that Epcot would have space for approximately twenty thousand residents. Two of the more interesting aspects of the Epcot plans were that all residents would (1) rent their respective living spaces (there would be no property owners) and (2) be required to work on Disney property (including the industrial park). By working on Disney property, Walt hoped that residents would feel a sense of community and thereby be invested in the city itself. The benefit of the "rental" component was that Disney could periodically update the technologies and products in the living units as newer versions of each became available.

While the goals and aspirations for the "city of tomorrow" were admirable, they were not without criticism. One such criticism involved the privacy (or lack thereof) of the individuals and families living in Epcot's residential areas. As discussed by author Steve Mannheim in one of the definitive guides on the initial conceptual plans for Epcot, *Walt Disney and the Quest for Community* (2002), this concern was brought directly to Walt Disney's attention:

> Disney advisor Ray Watson recalls that he raised the issue directly to Disney in 1966, saying, "Now, you're not going to go out and get it [the milk] in your pajamas. You're going to have to dress up and put a tie on because these people that live there are now on exhibit, just like your cast members are elsewhere." Putting himself in an EPCOT resident's place, Watson envisioned visitors peering down at his house from PeopleMovers and told Disney just that. While the EPCOT concept remained at a conceptual stage at the time of Disney's death, Watson's concern was a real one; EPCOT's goals of being both a showcase and a community dedicated to the needs of residents may not have been compatible.

Notwithstanding these and other criticisms, the Epcot film is quintessential Disney, and conveys an innovative concept in a warm and gentle manner. In closing the film, Walt recognized the enormous scope of the Epcot project while also maintaining a sense of confidence about his ability to meet that challenge:

> That's the starting point for our Experimental Prototype Community of Tomorrow. And now where do we go from these preliminary plans and sketches? Well, a project like this is so vast in scope that no one company alone could make it a reality. But if we can bring together the technical know-how of American industry and the creative

> imagination of the Disney organization, I'm confident we can create—right here in Disney World—a showcase to the world of the American free enterprise system. I believe we can build a community that more people will talk about and come to look at than any other area in the world and, with your cooperation, that the Experimental Prototype Community of Tomorrow can influence the future of city living for generations to come. It's an exciting challenge, a once-in-a-lifetime opportunity for everyone who participates.

## Walt Disney's Death

In 1966, Walt Disney experienced a variety of health problems including pneumonia and kidney trouble. The people who worked closest with Walt noticed several changes in him, most notably that Walt's previously unmatched energy was fading lower and lower. Unfortunately, there was a heartbreaking reason behind this. In November 1966, Walt received the devastating news that he had lung cancer. After having a lung removed, and only weeks from his initial diagnosis, Walt Disney suddenly died on December 15, 1966. This monumental loss cannot be understated. Walt's death was felt not only within the Disney organization but also across the world. For the company, the loss of its creative leader was nothing short of devastating and left the entire Florida Project in a state of flux.

Walt's older brother Roy, who had attempted to retire several times, once again postponed his retirement to move the Florida Project forward. Roy famously insisted that the project be renamed "Walt Disney World" in order to honor his younger brother and Walt's dreams for the Florida Project.

Despite Roy's loyal dedication, he was at heart a pragmatic realist. As the "businessman" of the Disney brother's partnership, he understood that, at the end of the day, the Disney theme parks were businesses that needed to make money. Based on this view, Roy pulled many employees off of the Epcot research and development team following Walt's death and focused on the Phase One plans for the Florida Project, most notably the Magic Kingdom.

Looking back from today's perspective, Walt's plans for Epcot essentially died with him. In *Walt Disney's Imagineering Legends and The Genesis of the Disney Theme Park* (2008), Jeff Kurtti recounts a story of Imagineer Marvin Davis, who worked tirelessly with Walt in conceptualizing the Epcot project, about the significant impact of Walt's death on that project:

> When [Walt's death] happened, there was a big meeting that included [WDP executive vice president and chief operating officer] Card Walker, [de facto studio head] Bill Anderson, and [CEO] Roy [O.] Disney. This meeting was in a big room, and to the best of my ability

> I presented Walt's concepts for EPCOT. I got through, and sat down, and Roy turned around and looked at me and he said, "Marvin... Walt's gone."

## What Are We Going to Do About Epcot?

To say that the Florida Project was a massive undertaking is a vast understatement. At the time, it was the largest private construction project in the world. Because of the substantial time and resources required to develop what would become known as Walt Disney World, the company divided its efforts into phases. Phase One would take place over an initial five-year period and would focus on development of the Magic Kingdom, a Disneyland-style park dedicated to fun, adventure, and fantasy for the entire family; a series of highly-themed resort hotels; and a variety of other ancillary entertainment options. Walt's dream of constructing Epcot would take place in Phase Two, after the Phase One projects were up, running, and generating revenue. The Disney company clarified this approach in its 1967 Annual Report:

> The enormous complexities of building an entire city—especially one that will always be a "blueprint for the future" and a perpetual showcase for American free enterprise—will require the cooperation of major American industry and considerable research and development before it is undertaken as part of the "second phase" of Walt Disney World. However, it has already elicited the interest and enthusiasm of many of America's major corporations; a number have assigned "task forces" to work with WED Enterprises in the determination and development of systems and materials that can be applied in EPCOT.

The Magic Kingdom officially opened on October 1, 1971, and quickly became a runaway success with attendance numbers steadily increasing throughout the first few months the park was open. Sadly, Roy O. Disney died just two short months after the Magic Kingdom opened.

In 1971, Disney published *The Story of Walt Disney World, Commemorative Edition: A Behind-the-Scenes Visit to the Vacation Kingdom*, a large promotional booklet about Walt Disney World. It provided the history of the Florida Project and a preview of the attractions and experiences that the Magic Kingdom would offer. The booklet is packed with large pictures, including many construction photographs of the entire property, with a clear emphasis on the Magic Kingdom. It is clear that the original plans for Epcot were still on the table in 1971, as the very last page of the booklet features a beautiful artistic rendering of the city of tomorrow. The picture looks like something straight out of a science-fiction film, with the unmistakable marquee hotel at the center of the proposed development rising like a glacier above the surrounding city. The booklet included the below narrative:

> **The Future World...**
>
> Walt Disney World is dedicated not only to how people play, but also to how they live and work. As part of the second phase of its development, Walt Disney envisioned a city...a world of the future planned as an example for today's world.
>
> "There's enough land here to hold all the ideas and plans we can possibly imagine," Walt Disney said in announcing the project. And in the Master Plan for these 43 square miles, he incorporated the ideas and philosophies of a lifetime.
>
> Central to these plans is the community Walt Disney called EPCOT—Experimental Prototype Community of Tomorrow—"where people actually live a life they can't find anywhere else in the world today."

Strangely, the Epcot portion of the Florida Project was rarely mentioned or discussed by Disney in the years that followed. In the mid-1970s, however, Disney executives and Imagineers began asking the inevitable question: what do we do next?

The 1974 Annual Report for Walt Disney Productions included a two-page discussion of the Experimental Prototype Community of Tomorrow, stating in part:

> From the outset of planning and through the design, construction and installation stages of Walt Disney World, EPCOT has been the ultimate goal, as evidenced by the innovative systems, devices, materials and construction techniques already in use there.
>
> However, 1975 will mark the first period of concentrated planning and design for the "centers of activity" within EPCOT itself. Wide-ranging discussions will be held with representatives of world governments, leading businessmen, engineers, scientists and artists, for only through their cooperation will the Company be able to bring this immense concept to life.

Card Walker's "report" that accompanied the 1975 Annual Report for Walt Disney Productions proclaimed that "we are ready to move forward with confidence to the realization of Walt Disney's greatest dream." It also provided more insight on where the practical plans for Epcot were moving:

> We believe that in order to attain Walt Disney's goals for EPCOT, we must avoid building a huge, traditional "brick-and-mortar" community which might possibly become obsolete, in EPCOT terms, as soon as it is completed. We believe we must develop a community system oriented to the communication of new ideas, rather than to serving

the day-to-day needs of a limited number of permanent residents.

From this it appears that Walt's original goal of having actual residents live in the "Epcot City" were already fading away in 1975.

## Moving Forward with Epcot as a Theme Park Concept

Disney executives began to wrestle with a couple of different hurdles regarding the Epcot plans as envisioned by Walt. First, was a utopian city even a feasible concept that could be developed, constructed, and maintained? Second, and perhaps even more important, how would Disney make a commercial profit on Epcot, especially given the enormous capital investment that would be required to even attempt it?

Disney executives and Imagineers did not take the task of creating a viable concept for the Epcot project lightly. They spent the next several years developing, changing, re-developing, and re-changing different plans for what Epcot would actually be. According to Marty Sklar, Disney coordinated a series of "Epcot Future Technology Conferences" between 1976 and 1983 where Disney brought together their own executives and Imagineers with leaders from different industries including agriculture, energy, health, and space. The goal of these conferences was to inspire interest from leaders in relevant fields in Epcot and to develop a conceptual framework and a body of advisors for shaping the Epcot project.

The 1977 Annual Report for Walt Disney Productions provided insight about the thought process behind Epcot's development:

> As conceived here, EPCOT will be a "showcase for prototype concepts," demonstrating practical applications of new ideas and systems from creative systems everywhere. It will provide an "on-going forum of the future," where the best thinking of industry, government and academia is exchanged to communicate practical solutions to the needs of the world community. It will be a "communicator to the world," utilizing the growing spectrum of information transfer to bring new knowledge to the public. Finally, EPCOT will be a permanent "international people-to-people exchange," advancing the cause of world understanding.
>
> In addition, we are convinced that EPCOT will provide a much-needed symbol of hope and optimism that our major challenges can and will be met. It will provide outstanding family entertainment from which people may draw enlightenment, as well as enjoyment. And it will, of course, represent a major new extension of our business activities around the world.

On October 2, 1978, Card Walker, the president and chief operating officer of The Walt Disney Company (at the time known as Walt Disney Productions), spoke before the International Chamber of Commerce. Among the many other distinguished guests at this event was then-President of the United States Jimmy Carter. During Walker's speech, he announced that Disney would in fact be moving forward with the EPCOT Center project:

> Today, with enormous enthusiasm and excitement we are announcing that EPCOT Center—a vast new project for public interface with the concepts of tomorrow—will open October 1, 1982. This new project will be located just two miles from the Contemporary Resort Hotel and will be linked to the present Vacation Kingdom by Monorail.
>
> At a cost approximating one-half billion dollars, EPCOT Center will consist of two major themed areas: Future World and the World Showcase. The first of these will dramatize the history and future challenges of the critical problems facing us today—providing a public window onto the worlds of energy, transportation, the land, the seas, space, life and health and other subjects....
>
> The World Showcase will be a "community of nations," the only permanent international exposition of its kind anywhere, focusing on the culture, traditions, tourism and accomplishments of people around the world.

## Two Parks?

As Walker made clear, plans for Epcot now called for two separate and distinct theme park concepts. First, a World Showcase park would feature different pavilions themed to the architecture, history, and culture of a variety of nations across the globe. Second, a Future World park would consist of pavilions dedicated to human achievement and advancement in areas such as communication, energy, and imagination.

How did these two separate theme park concepts become one? According to Sklar, it was a quick decision made by he and Imagineer John Hench shortly before a meeting with Disney executives. Because of sponsorship troubles for both Future World and World Showcase, Sklar and Hench literally pushed the two models together in the hopes that the combined sponsorship dollars would be enough to fund one park. It worked!

This concept was even referenced as far back as 1976 in Card Walker's letter to shareholders that accompanied the 1976 Annual Report of Walt Disney Productions:

> ...by bringing together our "World Today" and "Future World" concepts into one major EPCOT Center, we can increase our initial sales

> potential to sponsors (countries and companies), place the beginning emphasis on achieving the most in the shortest time frame, create a permanent exposition for which a main gate admission will be charged, reduce substantially the capital investment which otherwise would have been required to construct transportation systems, utilities and service facilities to serve two separate attractions, guarantee substantially higher projections of attendance for the corporate sponsors of technology exhibits, and accomplish a design that will allow sufficient room for future growth in both parts of the EPCOT Center.

What was the real reason for drastically changing the plans for Epcot from a living, breathing, and working city into a theme park that combined two almost completely unrelated concepts? Opinions on that differ greatly. Some feel that the idea of a utopian city was simply not a feasible project in terms of construction, community regulation and oversight, and the constant need for evolution and upkeep. Others feel that, given the substantial financial investment that would have been required to get the project off the ground, Disney was just not willing to take that significant financial risk. And others simply think that the Disney leadership left in the wake of Walt's death could not come to grips with exactly what to do about the "city of tomorrow" concept without Walt's passion and leadership. The true reason is probably a combination of all of the above.

Epcot officially opened to guests on October 1, 1982. The Epcot Dedication Plaque explains the goals of the restructured park concept:

> Epcot is inspired by Walt Disney's creative vision. Here, human achievements are celebrated through imagination, wonders of enterprise and concepts of a future that promises new and exciting benefits for all.
>
> May EPCOT Center entertain, inform and inspire and above all, may it instill a new sense of belief and pride in man's ability to shape a world that offers hope to people everywhere.

## Remembering the City of Tomorrow Today

Although Walt's vision of Epcot never came to be, guests can still see bits and pieces of these plans throughout Walt Disney World. While guests cannot ride a monorail through an airport, industrial park, or utopian city en route to the Magic Kingdom, they can ride a monorail between Epcot and the Magic Kingdom and around the Seven Seas Lagoon past Disney's Grand Floridian Resort & Spa, Disney's Polynesian Village Resort, and Disney's Contemporary Resort. Guests can also enjoy a peaceful and relaxing ride on the Tomorrowland Transit Authority PeopleMover (formerly known as the WEDWay PeopleMover), which originally opened on July 1, 1975, in the Magic Kingdom. The PeopleMover gently weaves around and through the various attractions and buildings in Tomorrowland.

In 1967, a dramatic and intricately detailed one-eighth inch to the foot model that became known as the Progress City model was featured on the second level of the Carousel of Progress in Disneyland. In *Walt Disney and the Quest for Community* (2002), Steve Mannheim described the enormity of the Progress City model:

> It was incredibly detailed: it measured 6,900 square feet (115 feet wide), contained 22,000 miniature trees and shrubs, 4,500 buildings (lit from within), 1,400 street lights, a climate-controlled center city, amusement park rides in motion, sports stadiums, an airport, an atomic power plant, underground passageways, residential cul-de-sacs, retail establishments, monorails, electric sidewalks, schools, churches, electric trains, electric carts, and PeopleMovers.

In another definitive conceptual Epcot book, *Walt Disney and the Promise of the Progress City* (2014), Sam Gennawey quotes Imagineer Marty Sklar in describing the relationship of the Progress City model to Epcot: "That model almost exactly matched all our planning for EPCOT. I think Walt got a kick out of doing that model, without having to say that he was going to build this big city, but it was all there for anybody to see."

In 1975, the Carousel of Progress changed homes, moving from Disneyland to the Magic Kingdom where the attraction continues to entertain guests today. In this process, a portion of the Progress City model also moved to Tomorrowland and can be seen, appropriately enough, on the Tomorrowland Transit Authority PeopleMover attraction.

Vestiges of Epcot's original concept can also be found in the master planned community of Celebration, Florida. Celebration is a residential community featuring numerous amenities including walking trails, a golf course, and many retail shopping and dining options. Although Celebration does not feature monorails or PeopleMovers and residents do in fact own their own homes, the community does feature a greenbelt recreational area and very strict architectural and structural guidelines that homes must follow. Celebration welcomed its first residents in June 1996.

CHAPTER SEVEN

# The World Showcase That Never Was

*There is an ever-expanding number of pavilions to be incorporated into the World Showcase complex, some already in the planning stages.*

— Richard R. Beard, *Walt Disney's Epcot Center, Creating the New World of Tomorrow* (1982)

Epcot's World Showcase is one of the most unique theme park areas in the entire world. Where else can guests enjoy the culture, atmosphere, cuisine, and entertainment of eleven different nations in a single afternoon while travelling little more than one mile in the process?

World Showcase is themed as a permanent world's fair, with a wide variety of intricately detailed pavilions surrounding a forty-acre lake, the World Showcase Lagoon. Each of the eleven World Showcase pavilions is dramatically themed to a particular nation, and provides rich representations of the host countries' architecture, restaurants, shops, and entertainment. In addition, the cast members who work in each of the World Showcase pavilions are natives of the country represented, adding to the authenticity of the experience.

While thousands of Walt Disney World guests visit Epcot each and every day, few know that initial plans for World Showcase contemplated that it would be a stand-alone theme park. In addition, had history gone just a bit differently, World Showcase would have been home to a variety of additional national pavilions, including Equatorial Africa, Israel, Costa Rica, Iran, and the Soviet Union.

## A Standalone Park and Indoor Pavilions

The initial plans for World Showcase were dramatically different than what guests experienced on Epcot's opening day, October 1, 1982. In fact, the earliest designs for World Showcase contemplated that it would be a completely separate park!

The 1974 Annual Report for Walt Disney Productions included a captivating illustration of an early design for World Showcase. Amazingly, this illustration shows a stand-alone World Showcase park sitting on the shores of the Seven Seas Lagoon in approximately the same area as the Transportation and Ticket Center sits today. The Magic Kingdom, Disney's Contemporary Resort, and Disney's Polynesian Village Resort are also depicted in this illustration, with World Showcase connected to all of them by monorail.

The World Showcase concept evolved and was eventually incorporated into the designs for Disney's next major theme park, Epcot (at the time referred to as EPCOT Center). However, instead of eleven outdoor pavilions spread around a large lagoon, conceptual renderings called for two enormous semi-circular buildings that would each be divided into different segments, like pieces of a pie, for each participating country. Yes, you are reading that correctly, all of the national pavilions were to be housed completely indoors.

Each building would have had a clean, modern, and futuristic façade. All nations represented would have equal frontage from the exterior of the semi-circular structures. However, the interiors of each pavilion would be unique and richly themed. The sizes of each pavilion would vary from country to country based upon the particular plans for that nation and the amount of sponsorship dollars available to assist with the substantial costs of construction and operation of the pavilions.

The 1975 Annual Report to the shareholders of Walt Disney Productions included the following description of the conceptual framework for World Showcase:

> It will consist of a coordinated series of national pavilions housed side-by-side in two dramatic, semi-circular structures. These dynamic structures will face each other across a Courtyard of Nations where there will be a major theater for performances by international celebrities and entertainment groups, and where parades, pageants and special events will be staged by entertainers from the participating nations.
>
> Although these national pavilions may vary in size, each will enjoy equal façade exposure to the guest. The entire complex will be tied together by a Disney people-moving system that will offer visitors a preview look into each attraction.
>
> Unlike a world's fair, it will offer participating countries a permanent installation for such features as themed restaurants and shops,

product exhibits, industrial displays, cultural presentations, a trade center, and even special facilities for business meetings.

As noted in the above description, the semi-circular structures would face each other, creating a large Courtyard of Nations featuring several water features and a lengthy row of tall flagpoles, with each of the constituent countries' flags displayed. The courtyard would allow for a variety of guest entertainment options, including parades, special events, and musical performances, and would have also included a large "Observation Tower" at its center. Notably, these plans called for upwards of thirty different nations to be represented in World Showcase.

Eventually, the indoor pavilion concept for World Showcase was scrapped. In *Walt Disney Imagineering, A Behind the Dreams Look at Making the Magic Real* (1996), the rationale for this decision was explained as follows:

> Although sound in theory, the layout did not allow the designers to visually capture the ethnic essence of each of the participating countries. So the focus turned to the rich architectural diversity of each country. Each pavilion could be designed to present a look and style that reflected its ethnic architectural heritage. Not only would the pavilions be more visually exciting from afar, they would be immediately recognizable as the country each represented.

The 1977 Annual Report of Walt Disney Productions provided clarity on the new World Showcase design:

> In this new interfacing design concept, countries from around the world will stand side-by-side in friendship along the banks of a broad lagoon...symbolic of the waters that bind together the diversified peoples of the world.

This general description of World Showcase is what was actually constructed and opened to guests on October 1, 1982, with a series of pavilions surrounding the World Showcase Lagoon.

## Placement of World Showcase

When guests enter Epcot today, they pass through the turnstiles and enter Future World, a land dedicated to human achievement, science, and technology. Future World consists of a series of pavilions focusing on concepts such as communication, energy, agriculture, and imagination. World Showcase sits at the rear of Epcot, with guests having to first travel through Future World in order to get to the eleven national pavilions. However, as strange as this may sound today, early plans for Epcot contemplated that World Showcase would serve as the entry point of the park, not Future World.

Once Disney executives and Imagineers decided that Epcot would consist of two separate theme park areas, they believed that the true star of the park would be World Showcase. Perhaps "star" is the wrong word, but Disney did feel that the greatly needed sponsorship dollars would be easier to obtain for national pavilions than for pavilions themed on different scientific and technological concepts. This initial plan reflects how strongly Disney executives felt about their ability to obtain funding for World Showcase.

Imagineers anticipated that World Showcase would draw guests into Epcot, with the science- and technology-based Future World pavilions serving a secondary role in the back of the park. However, as we'll soon see, obtaining sponsorship funding for World Showcase pavilions proved much more difficult to obtain than Disney originally contemplated. Instead, sponsorship dollars for Epcot came in the form of Future World investments from companies such as Exxon, Kraft, and General Electric. Because of this, Disney executives were forced to change their plans for Epcot's layout. The focus turned to Future World, and the layout of Epcot was modified to what guests experience today, with Future World at the entrance of the park and World Showcase occupying the rear.

## World Showcase Pavilions That Never Were

In addition to the physical layout and location of World Showcase, the constituent nations represented therein also dramatically changed from what Disney executives initially contemplated.

Given that there are hundreds of nations in the world, you might be wandering how the eleven pavilions represented in World Showcase today were chosen. Was it geographic locale? Cultural diversification? Population? Religious representation? All of those factors undoubtedly played a part, but at the end of the day, the dominant factor was cold hard cash. Disney expected significant sponsorship dollars to help cover the substantial costs and expenses involved with constructing and operating the World Showcase pavilions. In the 1975 Annual Report to the shareholders of Walt Disney Productions, the critical role of funding for World Showcase was described as follows:

> Each participating nation will be asked to provide the capital to cover the cost of designing, developing and constructing its attraction and/or ride and all exhibits, as well as the Pavilion itself.... Its land lease will cover the cost of maintaining the attraction for a minimum of ten years.

Disney anticipated receiving sponsorships either from the governments of the respective nations or from major corporate entities in those countries. In exchange for their substantial investment, the host nations would have the opportunity to display their culture to thousands of theme park guests who, after getting a taste of the nations' culture, might decide to visit the real thing in the future. The Disney company would provide transportation systems and utilities for World Showcase, the Courtyard of Nations, and a central theatre.

In 1977, Walt Disney Productions CEO Card Walker sent a letter to the company's shareholders outlining a list of potential nations to be represented in World Showcase. It read in part:

> Our efforts have included Canada, Costa Rica, England, Israel, Japan, Mexico, Morocco, Poland, Saudi Arabia, South Korea, United Arab Emirates, Venezuela, West Germany, and other countries. Several of these have already indicated their intention to participate as sponsors of pavilions and exhibits in the World Showcase. Others are in varying stages of negotiations which we feel will lead to their participation.

It is clear that Disney anticipated having a wide variety of nations represented in World Showcase. However, the company soon discovered that obtaining sponsorship funding for particular pavilions was much more difficult in practice than in theory. Disney executives were forced to make educated guesses about which pavilions should be included in World Showcase, beginning construction of those pavilions, and then going after sponsorship dollars during the construction process.

Most of the corporate and national sponsorships received by Disney were minimal at best. Disney had to cover the bulk of these costs and expenses and, as a result, tighten its belt about which pavilions to include in World Showcase and what attractions and experiences to incorporate into those pavilions. The number of national pavilions planned for the park, which by some reports reached more than forty, dropped lower and lower as sponsorship efforts continued to prove unsuccessful.

When Epcot finally opened on October 1, 1982, World Showcase included nine pavilions: Mexico, China, Germany, Italy, the American Adventure, Japan, France, the United Kingdom, and Canada. Morocco and Norway would not join World Showcase until 1984 and 1988, respectively. Notwithstanding this small number as compared to initial estimates, a series of billboards placed throughout World Showcase promised three additional pavilions in the near future: Equatorial Africa, Spain, and Israel.

## Equatorial Africa

Of all the proposed World Showcase pavilions that never came to be, plans for Equatorial Africa were by far the most extensive, detailed, and beautiful. Had the Equatorial Africa pavilion been constructed, it could have been, along with the American Adventure, the centerpiece of World Showcase.

The nine opening day World Showcase pavilions represented nations from North America, Asia, and Europe. One of the glaring geographic omissions was Africa. Recognizing this, Disney executives placed a high priority on incorporating an Africa-based pavilion into World Showcase soon after the park opened.

Disney Imagineers Ken Anderson and Herb Ryman put together several detailed conceptual renderings for the Equatorial Africa Pavilion. Anderson, sometimes referred to as Disney's "jack of all trades," served as art director on classic Disney films such as *Snow White and the Seven Dwarfs* (1937), *Pinocchio* (1940), and *Fantasia* (1940) before working on Disneyland attractions such as Peter Pan's Flight and Mr. Toad's Wild Ride. Ryman was an accomplished Disney artist who created highly regarded artistic designs for Disneyland and Walt Disney World, including perhaps the most famous conceptual depiction ever produced of Cinderella Castle.

The Equatorial Africa Pavilion was to be located between the China and Germany Pavilions. It would have been different from the other World Showcase pavilions in that, rather than representing a single county, it would have showcased the history and culture of numerous African nations that lie across the equatorial belt, including Kenya, the Congo, Uganda, and Ethiopia. In his book *Walt Disney's Imagineering Legends* (2008), Jeff Kurtti quotes Anderson as stating "[a]nybody from any part of Africa, from sub-Sahara to South Africa, could claim at least one of these buildings as having been inspired by his area."

## Attractions and Experiences

A massive sixty-foot tall tree house was to serve as the visual centerpiece of the Equatorial Africa Pavilion. It was to be themed as a tree house created by African tribesman, and would have included a dramatic observation deck. As depicted in a 1983 illustration by Herb Ryman entitled "The Waterhole," guests standing on the deck could view a grand African watering hole with numerous species of wildlife including elephants, zebras, and giraffes stopping to have a drink at dusk. However, no actual animals would be used. Instead, the animals would be represented through a series of multi-sensory illusions created by Disney Imagineers. Through a combination of a dramatic film projected on a large screen, lighting effects, sounds, wind, heat, and smells, the Imagineers would have orchestrated an environment where guests believed they were standing above an actual African watering hole with wild animals drinking water just below their feet.

In *Walt Disney's Epcot Center, Creating the New World of Tomorrow* (1982), Richard Beard described the attraction:

> Its architectural motif is a tree house, in which visitors will overlook a jungle water hole in a simulated nighttime environment. The illusion

> of the jungle will be heightened by a remarkably authentic diorama of trees, vines, boulders, and rushing water; even the scents of the forest will be re-created. These actual objects, sounds and smells are blended skillfully with a rear-projected film of animals visiting the water hole to convince visitors that they are actually in the heart of Africa.

A richly African-themed environment would have surrounded the tree house with lush landscaping and numerous thatched roof huts scattered throughout the area.

Disney partnered with Pulitzer-Prize winning author Alex Haley to consult on the Equatorial Africa Pavilion and to help create another guest experience known as Africa Rediscovered. The involvement of Haley, the author of the culturally significant novel *Roots*, gave the pavilion generally and Africa Rediscovered specifically instant credibility.

Africa Rediscovered would have been a film narrated by Haley to provide an entertaining and dramatic portrayal of African history and culture. One of the more important goals of the film was to educate guests about the true history and culture of Africa and the African people and to combat the misguided perception of a primitive culture of uneducated tribes fighting wild animals on a daily basis.

A third guest experience known as the Heartbeat of Africa was to be the heart and soul of the Equatorial Africa Pavilion. The show would be set in a highly themed amphitheater featuring African-styled musical instruments coming to life and playing for park guests. The show was the brainchild of Ken Anderson and would have been an upbeat experience with drums (the heaviest influence), flutes, bells, horns, rhythm, lights, and excitement all combining to celebrate the rich musical culture and heritage of Africa.

The Heartbeat of Africa would have celebrated the past, present, and future of Africa, and would "culminate with an outdoor jazz concert filmed in a modern African city, the excitement building up as superimposed laser images begin to emanate from the instruments themselves." The name for the attraction comes from the idea that the show embodies how music is the "heartbeat" of Africa, as it permeates many facets of African life.

The Equatorial Africa Pavilion would have also included a Sound Safari, a unique auditory attraction where guests would walk through a heavily landscaped area with lush flora providing a visual barrier. Behind the foliage, a variety of animal sounds would echo from all directions, triggered by guests passing infrared sensors. To support the illusions, plants would rattle and shake to coincide with the animal sounds to make guests believe that elephants, hippos, and other wild animals were just behind the jungle landscape. The attraction would ultimately culminate in a cave setting with a pride of lions engaging in a feeding frenzy.

In addition to these attractions and experiences, Equatorial Africa would have provided numerous live entertainment options, with authentic African dancers, singers, and other talents performing throughout the pavilion. A richly detailed conceptual depiction of the Equatorial Africa Pavilion made by Herb Ryman in 1980 illustrates this energetic environment. Awash with earth tones, it shows an African village with numerous individuals performing a variety of dances.

The pavilion would have also included exhibits and displays of authentic African artwork, as well as unique shopping options allowing guests to purchase African folk art, woodcarvings, pottery, and a variety of brass, copper, and ceramic gifts.

## Promotion of the Equatorial Africa Pavilion

Disney executives were so sure that the Equatorial Africa Pavilion would be included in World Showcase that they promoted it in numerous ways. First, the television special of Epcot's grand opening that was hosted by Danny Kaye, *EPCOT Center: The Opening Celebration*, aired Saturday October 23, 1982, on CBS. It featured a segment with Kaye and Alex Haley dedicated to the Equatorial Africa Pavilion. The pair stood over a model of the pavilion while discussing it and ended the segment with a promise that the pavilion would be open "in about a year."

In 1982, Disney issued a promotional booklet entitled "EPCOT Center: A Pictorial Souvenir." It provided a comprehensive preview of the lands, attractions, and experiences that Disney's newest theme park would provide and featured a variety of conceptual renderings and designs. In addition to describing the World Showcase pavilions scheduled to open with Epcot in 1982, the booklet featured a preview of three additional World Showcase pavilions that were "coming soon," including Equatorial Africa:

> The Equatorial Africa pavilion takes you on safari through a world of natural beauty and adventure. You'll view the drama of wild animals from the safety of a giant Calcedia tree. You'll feel the exciting energy of the "Heartbeat of Africa" show and sway to the jungle beat of the music and dance. Alex Haley, noted author of *Roots*, is your host for "Africa Rediscovered," an adventure uncovering Africa's ancient cultural heritage.

Disney also notified guests of the Equatorial Africa Pavilion, including its actual location, by placing a sign in World Showcase between China and Germany announcing the "FUTURE SITE" of the Equatorial Africa Pavilion. The billboard, which was visible to guests on opening day, October 1, 1982, read: "Feel the Heartbeat of Africa's Heartland...Africa A World of Beauty and Heritage."

So why did the Equatorial Africa Pavilion never come to be? Lack of funding, primarily. Disney approached several African countries about the possibility of sponsoring the pavilion. However, given the constant state of political upheaval prevalent throughout much of Africa during the 1980s, reaching a deal to fund the pavilion proved almost impossible. The one country that did provide serious consideration to funding the Equatorial Africa Pavilion was South Africa. However, the system of racial segregation in South Africa known as apartheid was still in place during this time. Understandably, Disney did not want to be associated with a sponsorship from South Africa. Given this lack of funding, plans for the Equatorial Africa Pavilion were eventually shelved.

## Finding Africa in Walt Disney World Today

Today, the prospects for an Equatorial Africa Pavilion joining World Showcase are extremely low. This is not because the plans for the pavilion were not spectacular, or that such a pavilion would not be a fantastic addition. Instead, a land dedicated to Africa was included when Walt Disney World's fourth theme park, Disney's Animal Kingdom, opened on April 22, 1998. The Africa section of that park, represented by the fictional town of Harambe, provides a stunning depiction of African architecture, culture, food, and even an authentic safari adventure in the form of Kilimanjaro Safaris. In addition, many of the design concepts developed for the Equatorial Africa Pavilion "tree house" were later incorporated into the Tree of Life, the enormous visual landmark and park icon for Animal Kingdom.

Another dramatic representation of Africa, Animal Kingdom Lodge, opened on April 16, 2001, as a deluxe Walt Disney World resort themed as a traditional African village. It features numerous displays of authentic African art, as well as four breathtaking savannas where guests can view over two hundred different species of animals.

Northern Africa did eventually become a part of World Showcase on September 7, 1984, when the Morocco Pavilion opened between Japan and the American Adventure.

The only remnant of the proposed Equatorial Africa Pavilion in Epcot today is the Outpost, which consists of a few outdoor shopping kiosks and a couple of snack stands between the China and Germany Pavilions. The area is minimally themed as an African locale, but certainly nothing compared to what was proposed for the Equatorial Africa Pavilion.

Although the chances of seeing an Equatorial Africa Pavilion in the future are small, the area originally proposed for the pavilion between China and Germany is the largest open plot of available land in World Showcase. So, if Disney does decide to add another pavilion, this would be an ideal location.

# Israel

Israel was one of the earliest nations considered for inclusion in World Showcase and was very close to being constructed. In fact, Israel even signed an agreement with Disney regarding the creation of an Israel Pavilion.

As was the case with Equatorial Africa, Disney promoted an Israel Pavilion in a number of different ways. First, Disney erected a billboard in World Showcase announcing the "FUTURE SITE" of the Israel Pavilion. The billboard advertised: "The Old Meets the New in 'The Land of the Bible.'"

Israel was also announced as "coming soon" in *EPCOT Center: A Pictorial Souvenir* (1982), which described the pavilion as:

> The Menorah, symbol of the State of Israel, stands on a courtyard center, surrounded by buildings reflecting the rich balance of new and old. Walk through ancient Jerusalem to an amphitheater to hear performances of both classical and folk music. Sample native dishes under the shade of olive and cypress trees in the Israel pavilion.

The 1978 Annual Report for Walt Disney Productions included many details about the proposed Israel Pavilion. Olive and cypress trees would line the entrance and provide a peaceful gateway into Israel. An energetic courtyard would feature a large menorah and house numerous shops to create a bazaar-like atmosphere.

One of the most exciting aspects of the proposed Israel Pavilion would have been the eclectic mix of unique gift options available for guests, including clothing, jewelry, and rugs all themed to the culture of Israel and its geographic region. Israel's information center was to be themed as an ancient minaret (lighthouse).

Perhaps the most relaxing entertainment option in any World Showcase pavilion would have been an amphitheater modeled after the theatre at Caesarea, where musicians would perform classic Israeli music. Guests would also dine on native cuisine in an open-air restaurant.

Plans for the Israel Pavilion were still "in development" as of 1983. Unfortunately, those plans eventually fell through due to a number of factors, including significant security concerns. However, the primary reason the Israel Pavilion never came to be was lack of funding. When the sponsorship dollars promised by Israel never came, Disney pulled the plans for the pavilion from World Showcase, notwithstanding the significant marketing efforts used to promote it.

# Spain

Spain was the third pavilion announced as "coming soon" in *EPCOT Center: A Pictorial Souvenir* (1982). The booklet described the pavilion as:

> Take a spectacular journey through Spain by film to little-known and out-of-the-way vacation Edens. A ride attraction captures the country's passionate heritage and spirit in her arts. In a waterside restaurant, indulge in tapas, or Spanish-style finger food—a blend of varied ingredients but suitable for simple tastes. And browse the market places of striking contrast, from pueblo village to aristocratic opulence.

From that description, it's evident that the Spain Pavilion was to include an attraction focusing on the culture of Spain, as well as a restaurant offering tapas and a wide variety of other food and snack offerings.

Disney also notified guests of the impending arrival of the Spain Pavilion by placing a billboard near the Germany Pavilion announcing that location as the "FUTURE SITE" of Spain. The billboard announced: "Discover the Golden Land of Segovia Cervantes and Picasso.... Discover Spain."

Unfortunately, plans for the Spain Pavilion, like Equatorial Africa and Israel, did not materialize into an actual World Showcase pavilion. Although the Spain Pavilion never came to be, Epcot did get a small taste of what the proposed pavilion was to offer when the Spice Road Table restaurant opened in the Morocco Pavilion in 2014. Guests can now enjoy tapas-style cuisine in a very relaxing waterside restaurant on the shores of the World Showcase Lagoon.

## Iran

One of the more captivating ideas for World Showcase was a pavilion dedicated to Iran. The Iran Pavilion would have included a dramatic replica of Golestan Palace, a World Heritage site in the capital city of Tehran, as the pavilion's architectural centerpiece. Plans for the Iran Pavilion also called for a dark ride through the rich history of the Persian Empire. Also included was a lively and energetic shopping bazaar offering guests unique gifts including intricately detailed wood and brass products.

As Marty Sklar notes in *Dream It! Do It!* (2013), Disney executives even made a presentation about the proposed Iran Pavilion to the Shah in Tehran. The 1976 Annual Report for Walt Disney Productions included a picture of a World Showcase presentation with the following caption:

> THE WORLD SHOWCASE. In October, his Excellency Ardeshir Zahedi Ambassador of Iran, visited WED Enterprises to view concepts for an Iranian World Showcase pavilion.

Despite these efforts, the prospects for an Iran Pavilion in Epcot's World Showcase permanently sank when the Shah of Iran was overthrown in 1979 as part of the Islamic Revolution.

## Venezuela

A Venezuela Pavilion that was at one time proposed for World Showcase would have offered numerous eye-catching architectural features and guest offerings. A large statue of Simon Bolivar, the legendary Venezuela military commander and political leader who played a large role in establishing Venezuelan independence from Spain, would mark the entrance to the pavilion.

The 1976 Annual Report of Walt Disney Productions included a dramatic illustration of the proposed Venezuela Pavilion drawn by Imagineer Claude Coates (of Haunted Mansion fame). Coates spent more than fifty years with the Disney company and worked on numerous attractions for Disneyland, Walt Disney World, and Epcot.

The depiction of the proposed Venezuela Pavilion in the 1976 Annual Report shows that the pavilion would have included a central plaza flanked by a variety of shops and restaurants with a variety of flora and water features both surrounding and incorporated into a courtyard. Interestingly enough, and in contrast to the other World Showcase pavilions that focused on traditional architecture, Venezuela would have emphasized modern architectural features and façades.

The signature attraction for the Venezuela Pavilion, and one that could have challenged for best attraction in all of World Showcase, was an aerial tram ride through a dense, lush rainforest, including a dramatic waterfall representing Angel Falls, the world's highest uninterrupted waterfall.

Despite these grand plans, the Venezuela Pavilion never came to be. As was the case with so many other pavilions, a lack of sponsorship dollars was the primary reason it was never constructed.

## United Arab Emirates

In the late 1970s, plans for World Showcase included a proposed United Arab Emirates Pavilion that would have been themed as an opulent oasis in the middle of a desert landscape, paying homage to the rich culture and heritage of the Middle East. The 1977 Annual Report of Walt Disney Productions included a conceptual depiction of an "Arab World."

When Card Walker announced to the International Chamber of Commerce on October 2, 1978, the Disney company's plan to move forward with the Epcot project, he even went so far as to state that Disney had received a letter of intent from several nations regarding participation in World Showcase, including the United Arab Emirates. A transcript of Walker's speech was included with the 1978 Annual Report for Walt Disney Productions, which also included numerous details about the pavilion's offerings.

The entrance to the United Arab Emirates Pavilion would have been one of the most dramatic in any World Showcase pavilion, as guests would pass through two ancient Arabic dhows (sailing ships). Once inside, guests would encounter a Bedouin (nomadic Arab) encampment.

The centerpiece of the pavilion would have been a flying carpet attraction that took guests past various scenes of Arabic history and culture. A genie would serve as the narrator and guide. At one point, the "magic carpets" would even pass through a holographic genie. The narrator would explain to guests the substantial contributions of Arabic culture to the fields of mathematics, astronomy, navigation, science, and medicine. The attraction would culminate with an overview of current culture in the Arabic world. One can only imagine the significant intellectual property tie-ins that would have been possible between a United Arab Emirates Pavilion and Disney's 1992 classic animated film *Aladdin*...especially the hilarious Genie.

The shopping areas for the pavilion were to be themed as an Arabic bazaar, straight out of *Arabian Nights*, with numerous black tents offering goods featuring brass, wood, and other materials.

Unfortunately for theme park guests, the funds promised by the United Arab Emirates never materialized, and Disney eventually pulled the pavilion from its World Showcase plans.

## Costa Rica

After failing to obtain sponsorship funding for several pavilions, including the United Arab Emirates and Israel Pavilions, Disney focused its attention on Costa Rica. The 1979 Annual Report for Walt Disney Productions stated that "[v]arious stages of negotiations for World Showcase" included those with the Costa Rican government.

Spanish Colonial architecture would have set the mood in the Costa Rica Pavilion. As depicted in a pair of colorful 1979 conceptual illustrations by artists B. Ayers and Tom Gilleon, the Costa Rica Pavilion would have been home to Walt Disney World's second Crystal Palace. However, instead of a character dining location featuring Winnie the Pooh and his friends from Pooh Corner that guests experience in the Magic Kingdom, the Costa Rican version would have featured a grand botanical garden with lush vegetation, flowing waterfalls and waterways, and tropical birds displayed in a dramatic multi-level glass conservatory.

As a part of the planning process for the Costa Rica Pavilion, Disney Imagineers created a detailed model of the proposed pavilion. Unfortunately, as told by Disney historian Jim Korkis in his book *Secret Stories of Walt Disney World* (2015), the model strangely disappeared shortly after a presentation made to governmental officials and was never recovered.

When Costa Rica failed to supply the expected sponsorship dollars (you are probably noticing that is a recurring theme), Disney scrapped plans for the pavilion.

## Scandinavia/Denmark

Plans for a proposed Denmark Pavilion began even before the opening of Epcot in 1982. The 1980 Annual Report for Walt Disney Productions stated that designs were "now underway" for a Denmark Pavilion. After those initial plans were delayed, Denmark was slated for the second phase of World Showcase to be implemented after Epcot opened.

The Denmark Pavilion was slated to feature a number of unique experiences and guest offerings, such as an ice skating rink. But most important, Denmark would have included a recreation of Tivoli Gardens, a famous amusement park located in Copenhagen, Denmark, that first opened in 1843, with a grand carousel and Ferris wheel. One of the more interesting proposals was a canal ride that passed through miniature recreations of famous world landmarks made of...LEGOs.

The Denmark plans morphed into a multi-country Scandinavian Pavilion. In his letter to stockholders that accompanied the 1983 Annual Report of Walt Disney Productions, Ron Miller, the president and CEO, stated:

> WED Enterprises is now designing a Scandinavian showcase under a preliminary design agreement with Norwegian business interests. It will combine the cultures of Norway, Sweden and Denmark in another exciting World Showcase presentation.

Lack of sponsorship funding, among other reasons, killed both a Scandinavian Pavilion and a stand-alone Denmark Pavilion. But Disney did receive strong financial support from sponsors in Norway. As such, construction of a standalone Norway Pavilion began in World Showcase in 1986, and it officially opened in 1988.

## Philippines

Plans for a Philippines Pavilion in World Showcase were put together in the early 1980s. Claude Coates, as he had done with so many other pavilions, created initial designs for the Philippines. From these depictions we know that, upon entering the pavilion, guests would have been welcomed by an outrigger canoe with a large multi-colored sail floating in a pool of water.

Walking farther into the Philippines Pavilion, guests would have experienced a variety of different architectural styles, including a Spanish-styled two-story building with multi-level porches and walking paths, contrasted with thatched roof "hut"-style buildings.

At the rear of the pavilion, a large curved stage would have provided ample room for authentic Philippine music. The primary guest experience was to be a film highlighting the rich history and culture of the Philippines. A lively courtyard would provide a variety of shopping and dining options themed to an island atmosphere.

Plans were shelved when the Philippines government balked at the hefty price tag quoted by the Disney company for construction of the pavilion.

## Switzerland

Disney executives began negotiating with Swiss officials about a Switzerland Pavilion for World Showcase in the mid 1980s. The pavilion would have been themed as a quaint and romanticized Alpine village to be located between the Italy and Germany Pavilions.

Looming in the background of the Switzerland Pavilion would have been a visually breathtaking Matterhorn Mountain with a thrill ride similar to the Matterhorn Bobsleds in Disneyland. As the real Matterhorn Mountain is located in the Alps and straddles Switzerland and Italy, the inclusion of a replica of the Matterhorn in plans for a Switzerland Pavilion was a natural connection. The Disney company went so far as to announce this "Matterhorn Mountain bobsled ride" in its 1991 Annual Report.

As for the attraction itself, the Matterhorn was to be upwards of one-hundred-and-ninety feet tall, and would have provided a striking landmark for the pavilion visible from almost every corner of World Showcase. The attraction would have been a bobsled-style roller coaster. Unlike the Disneyland Matterhorn, the World Showcase version would have been completely enclosed in the mountain in much the same way as Space Mountain is enclosed in the Magic Kingdom.

The Switzerland Pavilion would have offered a variety of shops, including a clock shop, a wood-carving shop, and a Swiss snack shop. This does sound very familiar to some of the quaint shops offered in the Germany Pavilion today. The Switzerland Pavilion would have also included a restaurant offering breathtaking views of, among other things, the Matterhorn.

Unfortunately, Disney's negotiations with the Swiss government fell apart and plans for the pavilion, including the Matterhorn, never materialized.

## Soviet Union

The Disney Decade was a period of unprecedented growth for Disneyland and Walt Disney World spearheaded by chairman and CEO Michael Eisner. The Disney Decade saw the addition of numerous resort hotels, attractions, entertainment options, and experiences, including Splash Mountain, Muppet-Vision 3-D, and the Boardwalk Resort.

In 1990, Eisner announced the Disney Decade during a press conference at the Disneyland Hotel in California. During this presentation, he claimed that Disney was in negotiations with the Soviet Union for a Soviet Union Pavilion in World Showcase. In his letter to shareholders that accompanied the 1990 Annual Report of The Walt Disney Company, Eisner proclaimed that he had visited Moscow during the summer of that year "to persuade the Russians to help finance a Soviet pavilion at Epcot Center." Eisner did note, however, that he was "not sure what progress" he made during that visit.

As part of the planning process for the Soviet Union Pavilion, dramatic conceptual artwork was created by, among others, Claude Coates. Based on this artwork, we know that the Soviet Union Pavilion would have been perhaps the most visually stunning pavilion in all of World Showcase. It would have included its own Red Square with an awe-inspiring recreation of St. Basil's Cathedral, complete with the cathedral's enormous signature "onion domes" and large spires serving as the centerpiece of the pavilion.

The conceptual renderings also show that a large brick wall would have enclosed the pavilion, with an entrance at the front funneling guests into a massive courtyard. This stunning illustration was included in the 1991 Annual Report of the Disney company.

The signature attraction was to be Russia: The Bells of Change, an exciting concept combining audio-animatronics, music, film, and a live-action cast member that would "portray the volatile history of this vast land."

A second attraction, a dark ride, was to be based on the famous Russian folk tale "The Fool and the Fish." In this folk tale, a young "fool" named Ivan catches a magical pike. The fish promises Ivan as many wishes as he likes in exchange for its freedom. As is often the case with wish-based stories, Ivan's wishes initially cause trouble before eventually leading him to marry the tsar's daughter. This attraction would have been tailored toward children to balance the adult focused Bells of Change.

Along with these two attractions, the pavilion would have also offered a wide variety of entertainment and shopping experiences.

When the Soviet Union collapsed in 1991, plans for the World Showcase Pavilion collapsed with it. As Russia's economy would suffer for years to come, it became clear that there was little hope of receiving sponsorship dollars to construct the pavilion. Interestingly enough, the Russian economy has improved significantly in recent years, and with it the rumors of a Soviet Union addition to World Showcase have begun to swirl once more.

## Millennium Village

In 1999, as part of a special event to celebrate the new millennium, a large tent was erected in the large open space on the World Showcase promenade between the Mexico and Canada Pavilions. This tent became known as the Millennium Village, and featured several "mini-pavilions" for various countries that were not already represented in World Showcase.

*Walt Disney World Resort, A Souvenir for the Millennium* (1999), provided this description of the Millennium Village:

> Artisans, craftsmen, singers, dancers, and cultural representatives from dozens of countries fill the 65,000-square foot Millennium Village, celebrating the cultural achievement of nations never before seen at Epcot.

Some of the pavilions that had been proposed for inclusion in World Showcase but never came to be were represented in the Millennium Village. For example, Israel was featured as an exhibit that ran from 1999 through 2001. It included a motion-based simulator attraction known as Journey into Jerusalem, which provided a historic tour of various religious sites. Other nations in the Millennium Village included Chile, Eritrea, Saudi Arabia, and Scotland.

The Millennium Village continued for fifteen months before closing in January 2001. The space is now used for conferences, exhibitions, trade shows, receptions, and similar events.

## Final Take

It has been almost three decades since the last pavilion was added to Epcot's World Showcase. Unbeknownst to most theme park guests, there are at least six available plots of land in World Showcase where new pavilions could be added if the Disney company decided to do so.

Will we ever see a new nation in World Showcase? With an emphasis on adding new attractions, shows, hotels, and lands that will bring new visitors to each of the four theme parks, would a new national pavilion in World Showcase draw enough of these visitors to justify the expense? Those are difficult questions to answer. But if we have learned anything from Disney Imagineers, it is that good ideas never truly die. For now, guests will have to be content to stroll through the existing World Showcase pavilions and wonder what could have been.

CHAPTER EIGHT

# Epcot Entertainment Pavilion

*An idea can change tremendously during its development. Even though a story theme may remain true to its original spark to opening day, its physical design may experience hundreds, if not thousands, of alterations.*

— The Imagineers, *Walt Disney Imagineering, A Behind the Dreams Look at Making the Magic Real* (1996)

The above quote exemplifies one of the main themes of this book: great ideas never truly die. The amazing attractions, lands, and experiences developed by Disney Imagineers that, for a variety of reasons, never made it into Walt Disney World often persist as iterations of those original designs.

Perhaps the most extreme example of this theme was a proposed Entertainment Pavilion that Disney executives considered adding to Epcot's Future World in the 1980s. Although it didn't make it into Epcot, it evolved perhaps more so than any other proposed theme park concept that never came to be. In fact, plans for the Entertainment Pavilion not only morphed into a star-studded headliner attraction, but also into Walt Disney World's third major theme park.

## Something Missing in Epcot?

Shortly after Michael Eisner became the chairman and CEO of The Walt Disney Company in 1984, he immersed himself in all of the company's ongoing and proposed projects. One of these proposed projects, an Entertainment Pavilion for Epcot's Future World, was the brainchild of Imagineer Marty Sklar. Sklar's career with Disney spanned more than fifty years. His impressive resume includes work on classic Disney attractions such as It's a Small World and The Enchanted Tiki Room in addition to supervising other major projects for the company across the world.

In his book *Dream It! Do It!* (2013), he explained how the idea arose for an Entertainment Pavilion:

> When Epcot opened in October 1982—two years before [Michael] Eisner and [Frank] Wells came to Disney—our creative team at Imagineering began an analysis of subjects and stories we felt were missing from the Future World area [of Epcot].... In our own assessment, we found a glaring omission: there was no pavilion related to show business. Yes, the park itself was all about entertainment and fun—but what about exploring television, the Broadway stage, or how movies are made?

Based on this analysis, Sklar and his team developed plans for an Entertainment Pavilion that would pay tribute to the genres of cinema, television, theatre, and radio. *The Imagineering Field Guide to Disney's Hollywood Studios at Walt Disney World* (2010) explained that this proposed Entertainment Pavilion would have celebrated "entertainment as both an art form and a business."

## Entertainment Pavilion Offerings

Sklar's plans for the Entertainment Pavilion featured several separate and distinct components. First, the pavilion would include an attraction "that would take guests on a journey into the magic of the movies—literally." This attraction would have been the star of the pavilion and would have celebrated the genre of feature films and paid homage to numerous classic movies.

Although Imagineers believed that a "movie" attraction would be a great draw for park guests, the Entertainment Pavilion would have been much more than a single attraction. It would have also celebrated the entertainment genres of television and radio by virtue of a soundstage show experience and "a radio show that touted the importance of sound in storytelling." In addition to these experiences, plans for a Mickey's Movieland were also developed. This proposed attraction would tell the history of Mickey Mouse cartoons through various audio-animatronic scenes.

In terms of geographic location, the Entertainment Pavilion would have been located in Epcot's Future World between the Imagination Pavilion and the Land Pavilion behind the Innoventions West plaza.

So why did the Entertainment Pavilion never make it into Future World? Unlike most stories of Walt Disney World attractions that never came to be, where fans are sadly left to think about what could have been, Disney executives made the decision to expand the Entertainment Pavilion concept exponentially. Sklar explained:

> By the time we showed early concepts [of an Entertainment Pavilion] to Michael [Eisner] and Frank [Wells], we were all excited about its potential—and they quickly saw a new potential: why not place it outside but immediately adjacent to Epcot, and make it into a separate experience—perhaps a half-day park?

The decision to move forward with a standalone theme park dedicated to movies, television, theatre, radio, and all other elements of the entertainment industry were accelerated because Disney's rival, Universal Studios, announced that it was building a park in Orlando themed as a working movie and television studio. With that additional motivation, Disney quickly moved forward with construction of its third theme park officially called Disney-MGM Studios (later renamed to Disney's Hollywood Studios).

## Vestiges of the Entertainment Pavilion

Disney-MGM Studios opened on May 1, 1989, and became an instant success with visitors flooding the gates from the beginning. While the park as a whole represents a larger embodiment of the proposed Entertainment Pavilion, many of the specific experiences originally contemplated for that pavilion were also represented here. On opening day, the marquee experience was a "movie attraction" called The Great Movie Ride. Housed in a dramatic recreation of Grauman's Chinese Theatre (now known as the TCL Chinese Theater), the attraction takes guests on a journey through numerous tableaus of famous feature films from the 1930s through the 1980s, including *Singin' in the Rain* (1952), *Mary Poppins* (1964), *Raiders of the Lost Ark* (1981), *Casablanca* (1942), and *The Wizard of Oz* (1939). The Great Movie Ride continues to entertain guests today.

The television soundstage experience originally contemplated for Epcot's Entertainment Pavilion was represented in Superstar Television, another opening day attraction. Superstar Television allowed guests to see how live television programs were created by casting them in roles from popular shows such as *I Love Lucy* and *Gilligan's Island*. Those guests would perform their roles live on stage with cameras rolling and a live audience watching the performance. Superstar Television closed its doors in September 1998.

Finally, the radio show experience planned for the proposed Entertainment Pavilion morphed into the Monster Sound Show. This attraction allowed guests to perform a variety of audio effects for a short comedy film starring actors Chevy Chase and Martin Short. The Monster Sound Show entertained guests until 1997 when it changed to the ABC Sound Studio, which later became Sounds Dangerous, a show starring actor Drew Carey that focused on sound effects in the film industry. Sounds Dangerous closed in May 2012.

CHAPTER NINE

# Lost World Showcase Attractions

*After a period of incubation, which the Disney creative product has traditionally required, we are now, throughout the company, experiencing the excitement of seeing new projects move from the drawing board to reality.*

— 1977 Annual Report, Walt Disney Productions

Epcot's World Showcase is one of the most popular areas in all of Walt Disney World. Eleven distinctly themed pavilions celebrating the culture of a variety of nations are spread around the perimeter of a beautiful man-made lagoon. World Showcase is the perfect place for guests to enjoy exotic cuisine, breathtaking architecture, unique shopping experiences, and international entertainment. For all of its strengths, however, World Showcase is lacking in the number of attractions that guests can enjoy.

The eleven World Showcase pavilions collectively offer six attractions:

- Reflections of China
- Impressions de France
- O' Canada
- Gran Fiesta Tour Starring the Tree Caballeros in the Mexico Pavilion
- The American Adventure
- Frozen Ever After in the Norway Pavilion

Even that number is being generous, as three of those "attractions" are Circle-Vision 3D films in which guests are surrounded by nine large screens that create an immersive film experience.

Based on this list, it may come as a surprise to find out that original plans for World Showcase called for every national pavilion to include an attraction. The 1975 Annual Report of Walt Disney Productions made this clear by stating:

> A major part of each pavilion will be a Disney-designed ride or attraction which will give guests a foretaste of an actual visit to the country.

These lost World Showcase concepts are some of the most unique ideas ever conceptualized by Disney Imagineers. They include a roller coaster that travels through an exotic mountain peak, two tranquil boat rides down international rivers, speeding bullet trains, and even appearances by three Christmas ghosts from an 1843 Charles Dickens novel.

## Rhine River Cruise

The Germany Pavilion is one of the most colorful and boisterous pavilions in all of World Showcase. A statue of St. George slaying a dragon stands in the middle of a festive courtyard set within a perpetual Oktoberfest atmosphere. The Germany Pavilion features Biergarten, a table service restaurant themed as a simulated German town square complete with live music and yodeling, and Sommerfest, a counter service restaurant serving frankfurters and other quick bites. The pavilion also features an enticing caramel shop and stores that sell teddy bears, Christmas ornaments, and cuckoo clocks.

Even though Germany offers numerous offerings to keep guests both entertained and well fed, the pavilion does not feature an actual attraction. However, several years before Epcot opened, Imagineers were already developing plans for one to be included in the Germany Pavilion called the Rhine River Cruise. In fact, Card Walker's letter to shareholders that accompanied the 1976 Annual Report of Walt Disney Productions includes a reference to a "German Rivers Cruise" comparable to the very well-known It's a Small World attraction in the Magic Kingdom.

Of all the World Showcase attractions that never came to be, the Rhine River Cruise was probably the closest to becoming a reality. The attraction would have been a relaxing, slow-paced boat ride down a simulated version of the Rhine River that flows through the Swiss Alps and Germany, as well as other famous German waterways including the Tauber, the Ruhr, and the Isar Rivers. On this cultural and historical tour of Germany, guests would see miniature re-creations of the Ruhr Valley, the Black Forest, Rothenburg, Heidelberg, the Cologne Cathedral, and Neuschwanstein Castle (which has its own deep Disney roots since it is one of the many castles upon which Imagineers drew inspiration in designing Cinderella Castle for Walt Disney World).

Imagineer Harper Goff worked on the initial concept for the Rhine River Cruise. Goff's credits include extensive work on the classic 1954 Disney film *20,000 League Under the Sea*, as well as Disneyland's Main Street, U.S.A. and the Jungle Cruise attraction.

In 1976, Imagineer Sam McKim created a conceptual depiction of a piece of this proposed attraction entitled "Rhine River Cruise Queue." McKim was best known for his colorful Disneyland maps from the late 1950s and early 1960s, as well as his work on Pirates of the Caribbean, the Haunted Mansion, and the Carousel of Progress in Disneyland. Unfortunately, McKim's depiction of the Rhine River Cruise does not provide many substantive details, other than white passenger boats with canopies featured in the painting's background. The only "queue" depicted is a checkerboard floor with numerous guests milling about while a series of non-descript buildings are seen in the background under a nighttime sky.

Unlike many of the other attractions considered for inclusion in World Showcase, Disney actually began construction on the Rhine River Cruise, but the project was abandoned. However, curious guests can still see what would have been the entrance to the Rhine River Cruise when they dine at Biergarten or Sommerfest at the very back of the Germany Pavilion. The former would-be entrance is located underneath an arch on a wall with a large colorful mural depicting a German countryside.

## Proposed United Kingdom Attractions

The United Kingdom Pavilion is one of World Showcase's more quaint pavilions, with a blend of architectural styles and a number of unique shopping options, including a toy shop, a tea shop, and a place where families can buy gifts featuring their own coat of arms and...should the need arise... even a sword. Its biggest draw is the Rose and Crown Pub and Dining Room, a traditional English pub that serves up British favorites such as fish and chips and bangers and mash. For all of its good features, however, the pavilion does not feature an attraction to entertain guests. However, numerous attraction concepts have been proposed, including a journey through a famous Christmas story and a river cruise past London landmarks.

### A Christmas Carol

In the early 1980s, Imagineers considered adding a "full-scale Audio-Animatronics show" based on Charles Dickens' 1843 novel *A Christmas Carol*. In *The Art of Walt Disney World Resort* (2009), authors Jeff Kurtti and Bruce Gordon include three beautiful acrylic paintings by Imagineer Sam McKim of proposed scenes from this Dickens'-based attraction. "Are You the Spirit, Sir, Whose Coming Was Foretold to Me?" depicts a frightened Ebenezer Scrooge cowering beneath the sheets in his bed as a glowing Ghost of Christmas Past peers down from a nearby fireplace mantle.

"A Jolly Giant, Glorious to See" depicts "a melding of Christmas symbology, including Santa Claus, a Christmas tree, and the Ghost of Christmas

Present." This painting shows Ebenezer Scrooge peering over the side of his bed, which is floating high in the air. The Ghost of Christmas Past, who is represented as half Santa Claus and half Christmas tree, laughingly stares back at the frightened Scrooge.

The third and final McKim depiction entitled "The Last of the Spirits" provides the spookiest and most chilling look at the proposed Dickens attraction. A sinister Ghost of Christmas Yet to Come, clad in a long black robe, points Scrooge to his own tombstone. The stingy miser stands in terror, surrounded by a cold, snowy cemetery and numerous other snow-capped tombstones.

### Thames River Ride

Imagineers also considered adding an attraction to the United Kingdom Pavilion in the mid-1980s known as the Thames River Ride. This attraction would have been a "log flume" taking guests on a scenic tour of both the history and notable landmarks of jolly old London. On this journey, guests would pass by the Tower of London, the Big Ben clock tower, and the Houses of Parliament (Clark Griswold would have certainly approved).

Imagineer Harper Goff created a colorful 1986 illustration of the proposed Thames River Ride. Goff's rendering depicts guests in a large boat floating past the above-referenced London landmarks under a cloudy nighttime sky. As was the case with Germany's proposed Rhine River Cruise, the Thames River Ride would have been a relaxing, entertaining, and educational experience for World Showcase guests.

Neither the Charles Dickens attraction nor the Thames River Ride was ever constructed. Information on why these concepts were abandoned is scarce. Financial pressures and a lack of corporate sponsorship dollars almost certainly played a role. However, given the significant Disney intellectual properties that have a connection to the United Kingdom, including *Mary Poppins* (1964), *Alice in Wonderland* (1951), *Robin Hood* (1973), and the characters from the *Winnie the Pooh* franchise, hope is always alive that one day the pavilion will finally get an attraction to entertain guests.

## Proposed Japan Pavilion Attractions

The Japan Pavilion, which sits between the American Adventure and the Morocco Pavilion, is one of the most picturesque and visually stunning areas in all of Walt Disney World. Among its many beautiful architectural features are a large red torii gate that sits in the World Showcase Lagoon, a magnificent five-story pagoda that is a replica of the 7th century Horyuji Temple, and the imposing White Heron Castle at the rear of the pavilion, modeled after a 17th century Japanese fortress. Despite the high architectural bar set by these structures, plans for the Japan Pavilion at one point included another massive structure that would have towered over the rest and completely changed the landscape of World Showcase as a whole: a Mt. Fuji roller coaster.

## Mt. Fuji Coaster

Imagineers considered adding a bobsled-type roller coaster attraction to the Japan Pavilion reminiscent of the Matterhorn Bobsleds, the famous roller coaster that first opened in Disneyland in 1959. Even more intriguing was that this attraction would have been set within a massive re-creation of Mt. Fuji, the highest mountain peak in Japan. As World Showcase has neither a thrill ride nor a "mountain" that would merit inclusion in the Disney "mountain range," a Mt. Fuji coaster would have been a unique addition to Epcot's offerings.

The 1991 Annual Report of The Walt Disney Company stated:

> Plans...were revealed to bring either a Matterhorn Mountain bobsled ride or a Mt. Fuji attraction to Epcot Center's World Showcase within the next five years. The Matterhorn would end in a Swiss village; Mt. Fuji would tower behind the Japan Pavilion.

So why did the Mt. Fuji coaster never come to be? During this time period, Eastman Kodak was a major sponsor for Epcot. Rumor has it that Kodak executives were not happy about a major attraction coming into Epcot that bore the name of their biggest rival, Fujifilm. Regardless of the reason, neither the Mt. Fuji structure nor the roller coaster to be included therein ever made it into the Japan Pavilion.

## Simulated Bullet Train Attraction

In addition to the Mt. Fuji concept, Imagineers considered an attraction based on Japan's famous network of Shinkansen trains (more commonly known as bullet trains) which travel at speeds upwards of two hundred miles per hour. The attraction would have used the familiar Disney Circle-Vision 3D screen system. Although World Showcase includes three such attractions already, the simulated bullet train ride would have been perhaps the most unique of these theatrical experiences.

This proposed attraction would have simulated travel in a passenger compartment for one of the famous high-speed Japanese bullet trains. Guests would have had the unique ability to look through oversized windows (which were not really windows) to see breathtaking images of Japanese landscapes and famous landmarks as the bullet train raced by. The simulated bullet train attraction would have also featured interactive elements such as vibrations to mimic those felt in the real trains.

The 1975 Annual Report of Walt Disney Productions included a conceptual rendering of the Japan Pavilion. As part of this illustration, a bullet train is shown exiting what appears to be a mountain. This depiction included a caption reading, "for discussion with Japan, national exhibits followed by a simulated high-speed train ride through the Japanese countryside."

Unfortunately, like the Mt. Fuji coaster, plans for a bullet train attraction in the Japan Pavilion were also shelved. Today, the closest that guests can get to travelling in a bullet train in Walt Disney World is to catch a ride on the Walt Disney World monorail which, thankfully, travels much slower than two hundred miles per hour.

PART THREE

# Disney's Hollywood Studios

*Another 1990 highlight was the January announcement and launch of the...Disney Decade, a program involving development and eventual construction of four new theme parks (our fourth in Florida and our second in Southern California, Japan and Europe), as well as 60 new projects in California and Florida, including new pavilions, attractions, hotels, rides, revues, adventures, extravaganzas and entertainment centers.*

— 1990 Annual Report, The Walt Disney Company

## CHAPTER TEN

# Roger Rabbit's Hollywood

*P-p-please, Eddie! Don't throw me out. Don't you realize you're making a big mistake? I didn't kill anybody. I swear! The whole thing's a set up. A scam, a frame job. Ow! Eddie, I could never hurt anybody. Oow! My whole purpose in life is to make...people...laugh!*

— Roger Rabbit, *Who Framed Roger Rabbit?* (1988)

Walt Disney originated the genre of animated feature films starting with *Snow White and the Seven Dwarfs* (1937). Over the next thirty years, Disney released many other classic animated movies including *Pinocchio* (1940), *Dumbo* (1941), *Bambi* (1942), *Cinderella* (1950), *Peter Pan* (1953), *Sleeping Beauty* (1959), and *The Jungle Book* (1967). Despite decades of success, Disney animation experienced a "dark age" during the 1970s and 1980s when both the quality and profitability of its animated films declined significantly.

The "Disney animation renaissance" refers to a roughly ten-year period following this "dark age" during which the business of Disney animation received a much-needed boost of creativity, innovation, writing quality, storytelling, and corresponding commercial success. According to Disney, this renaissance began in 1989 with the release of the blockbuster animated film *The Little Mermaid* and continued over the next decade with *The Rescuers Down Under* (1990), *Beauty and the Beast* (1991), *Aladdin* (1992), *The Lion King* (1994), *Pocahontas* (1995), *The Hunchback of Notre Dame* (1996), *Hercules* (1997), *Mulan* (1998), and *Tarzan* (1999). While no one can deny that the Disney animation renaissance included these films, an argument can be made that the renaissance did not begin with a beautiful mermaid named Ariel, but instead with a zany white rabbit named Roger.

A year before *The Little Mermaid* was released, *Who Framed Roger Rabbit?*, which combined both animation and live-action, took the world by storm. The film's starring character became a cultural phenomenon. How big of a phenomenon? Big enough that Disney planned on moving forward with an entire land in its newest theme park, Disney-MGM Studios, devoted to the world of Roger Rabbit.

Disney-MGM and *Who Framed Roger Rabbit?* was a thematic match made in heaven that was almost guaranteed to be an enormous financial success. So why did it never come to be? For once, the reason rested not with budgetary concerns, but instead with massive egos, Dick Tracy, and a deathly fear of spiders.

## Initial Groundwork for a Roger Rabbit Film

The mid-1980s was a tumultuous time for the Disney company, as it experienced a significant decline in overall revenues and battled multiple hostile takeover bids. As a result, its board of directors made a radical move that shifted the company's management structure. Ron Miller, Walt Disney's son-in-law and the head of the Disney studio, was asked to resign. On September 22, 1984, two new executives were installed to oversee the company's operations. Frank Wells, a former executive for Warner Bros., was named president and chief operating officer. Michael Eisner, the former head of Paramount Pictures, was named chairman and chief executive officer.

A few years prior to this massive corporate shake-up, Disney acquired the rights to the 1981 mystery novel *Who Censored Roger Rabbit?* by Gary K. Wolf. In the process of evaluating all active projects and proposed projects for Disney, Eisner made the decision to move forward with a film based upon the Wolf novel. However, Eisner recognized the substantial expense and risk involved with this endeavor, and looked for a partner to minimize the risk for the Disney company.

During his time as head of Paramount Pictures, Eisner developed a good relationship with director Steven Spielberg, whose credits include blockbusters such as *Jaws* (1975), *Close Encounters of the Third Kind* (1977), *Raiders of the Lost Ark* (1981), *E.T. The Extra Terrestrial* (1982), and *Back to the Future* (1985). Based on that relationship, Eisner negotiated a deal with Spielberg's production company, Amblin Entertainment, for a "partnership" between Disney and Amblin for development of a Roger Rabbit film. As a part of this deal, Spielberg and Amblin covered half of the cost and expense in making the movie, and in return were granted major creative powers and a significant cut of box-office and other revenues from the film and its characters. Most significantly for purposes of theme park additions, both Disney and Amblin would need to consent to any project involving use of the film's intellectual property rights, including the development of theme park attractions or a separate themed land based on Roger Rabbit.

Eisner viewed this relationship as having tremendous upside for the Disney company, opening the door for many future projects with

Spielberg. Eisner believed that the "consent" issue wasn't really an issue at all. According to Disney historian Jim Korkis, Eisner felt that Spielberg would "rubber stamp" any project that Disney proposed regarding Roger Rabbit due to Spielberg's primary focus on live-action films as opposed to animated films.

For Spielberg's part, his contributions to *Who Framed Roger Rabbit?* cannot be denied; in fact, many aspects of the film would not have been possible without Spielberg. Based on their relationship from the 1985 film *Back to the Future*, Spielberg retained Robert Zemeckis to direct *Who Framed Roger Rabbit?* Spielberg also brought in animator Richard Williams to lead the animation work. Perhaps most significantly, Spielberg was able to achieve what seemed at the time to be impossible: negotiating deals with numerous other studios that allowed for the use of their respective cartoon characters in the film for the small price of five thousand dollars per character.

## The Film

*Who Framed Roger Rabbit?* is set in the Golden Age of 1940s Hollywood, in a world where cartoons are actual living beings that interact with people on a day-to-day basis. These "toons" live in a city named Toontown, an animated suburb of Los Angeles. The story follows the misadventures of Roger Rabbit, a hyperactive, energetic, and fun-loving animated movie star. Roger is a white rabbit with long floppy ears, striking blue eyes, and red hair. His signature costume consists of bright red overalls and a blue bow tie with yellow polka dots.

In the film, R.K. Maroon, the head of the fictional Maroon Cartoon Studios, hires private investigator (and real person) Eddie Valiant to investigate why one of his biggest movie stars, Roger Rabbit, is having so many problems with his acting performances. The rumor going around Toontown is that Roger's wife, the seductive and voluptuous Jessica Rabbit (an animated woman), is having an affair with Marvin Acme, a prominent local businessman. When Acme is later murdered, all fingers (both real and animated) point to poor Roger. What follows is a madcap adventure through Hollywood and Toontown on a quest to clear Roger's name. Along the way, viewers meet the notorious Judge Doom, who presides over the superior court of Toontown and has developed a toon-killing substance known as "dip"; a group of villainous weasels that serve as Doom's henchmen; Baby Herman, a foul-mouthed, cigar-smoking baby; and Benny, a humorous animated taxicab. In the end, Valiant is able to clear Roger's name and uncover the plot of Judge Doom (who is really a cartoon in disguise) to destroy Toontown.

One of the most amazing aspects of *Who Framed Roger Rabbit?* is the finale, which features numerous animated characters from a wide variety of studios. Even today, almost thirty years following the film's release, I am always shocked to see the combination of characters such as Mickey Mouse, Minnie Mouse, Donald Duck, Bugs Bunny, Betty Boop, the Roadrunner, Wile E. Coyote, Porky Pig, and Droopy the Dog. It was a scene the likes of which we will never see again, and it would not have been possible without Stephen Spielberg.

*Who Framed Roger Rabbit?* featured a talented, albeit eclectic cast. Veteran actor Christopher Lloyd of *Back to the Future* fame voiced Judge Doom. Although several other more prominent actors were rumored to have been offered the part of Eddie Valiant (including Bill Murray), the role went to Bob Hoskins who would later star in the 1991 live-action Peter Pan-based movie, *Hook*. American standup comedian Charles Fleischer provided the voice of Roger Rabbit, and Kathleen Turner provided the seductive voice of Roger's wife, Jessica Rabbit. Turner was best known for her leading roles in 1980s films such as *Romancing the Stone* (1984) and *The Jewel of the Nile* (1985).

The film was released on June 22, 1988, through Touchstone Pictures, a Disney subsidiary. It quickly became an enormous critical and commercial success. Bringing in more than $300 million worldwide, it was the second highest grossing film of the year behind the Tom Cruise and Dustin Hoffman film *Rain Man*.

*Who Framed Roger Rabbit?* won three Academy Awards for Best Sound Editing, Best Film Editing, and Best Visual Effects. Richard Williams also won a Special Achievement Academy Award for his significant animation work on the film. Notably, *Who Framed Roger Rabbit?* was the first animated film since *Mary Poppins* (1964), over twenty years prior, to win multiple Academy Awards.

Even more important than awards and commercial success, the film made the public care about animation again. By any measure, *Who Framed Roger Rabbit?* was an overwhelming triumph and exceeded even the most ambitious expectations of the Disney company.

For its part, Disney knew that it had a blockbuster hit on its hands. The 1988 Annual Report for The Walt Disney Company is splattered with references to Roger Rabbit, including descriptions such as "stunning success," "spectacularly successful," "sophisticated," and "dazzling." Michael Eisner's letter to shareholders that accompanied the report reads more like a love letter to Roger Rabbit than a description of the financial state of the company. In an unprecedented move, the 1988 Annual Report even included a cutout of Roger!

## More Than a "Half-Day" Park

Disney-MGM Studios (now Disney's Hollywood Studios) opened on May 1, 1989. The park is devoted to movies, television, and entertainment, and is themed to replicate the glitz and glamour of Hollywood from the 1930s and 1940s, even including its own version of Hollywood Boulevard. This nostalgic feel was reflected in Michael Eisner's comments on the opening day of park, which are now reflected in its dedication plaque:

> The World you have entered was created by The Walt Disney Company and is dedicated to Hollywood—not a place on the map, but a state of mind that exists wherever people dream and wonder and imagine, a place where illusion and reality are fused by technological magic. We welcome you to a Hollywood that never was—and always will be.

Disney-MGM Studios was divided into two distinct sections, the first a theme park with attractions and shows that guests could enjoy on a daily basis, and the second an actual working studio where Disney filmed movies and television programming.

On the park's opening day, only a handful of attractions and experiences were in operation. Due to this limited number of guest offerings, and because half of the park was an actual working studio, Disney executives originally contemplated that the Disney-MGM Studios would only be a "half-day" park.

Notwithstanding these expectations, the park was an immediate success. Its streets were congested, lines for the few attractions and shows were long, parking lots were full, and the park had to regularly close to guests due to reaching capacity. Disney executives explained this success in their 1989 Annual Report:

> The huge crowds at The Disney-MGM Studios Theme Park on opening day were only the beginning. From spring through summer and into fall, attendance at this $500-million extravaganza outstripped the company's most optimistic estimates.
>
> In fact, within weeks Chairman Michael D. Eisner announced plans to double the park's entertainment segment—and its capacity—by 1993.

Due to this overwhelming guest demand, Disney executives began exploring options on how to expand the offerings at the park almost immediately. One of these options was to add an entirely new street that would intersect Hollywood Boulevard and that would bear the name of another famous California thoroughfare: Sunset Boulevard.

Today, Sunset Boulevard continues the theme of Golden Era Hollywood and is home to two of the most popular attractions in all of Walt Disney World: Twilight Zone Tower of Terror and Rock 'n' Roller Coaster Starring

Aerosmith. Early plans, however, called for a major Roger Rabbit presence on Sunset Boulevard. As described in the 1990 Annual Report for The Walt Disney Company:

> At the Disney-MGM Studios Theme Park, [new attractions and experiences] will star Roger Rabbit...and introduce park guests to such adventures as the Toontown Express....

## Welcome to Toontown

Based on the theme and time period of the Roger Rabbit film, which matched perfectly with the theme and time period of Disney-MGM Studios, Roger Rabbit seemed to be a tailor-made fit for the park. Imagineers began developing numerous concepts and ideas that would bring Roger and his co-stars into an entirely separate theme park land known as Roger Rabbit's Hollywood (although there were several different iterations of that name).

In terms of geographic layout, different versions of Roger Rabbit's Hollywood included both the entire length of the current Sunset Boulevard to a smaller location at the far end of Sunset Boulevard where the Rock 'n' Roller Coaster Starring Aerosmith is now located. The area would have replicated the wild and zany atmosphere of the film with gags, jokes, and tons of slapstick humor. An actual working Red Car Trolley would have transported guests down Sunset Boulevard and deposited them at a re-creation of the fictional Maroon Studios.

One of the things that makes Roger Rabbit's Hollywood so exciting to think about, and yet so disappointing that it never came to fruition, is that the area would have featured not one, not two, but three actual attractions. A 1990 *New York Times* article described the general plans for the Roger Rabbit expansion in Disney-MGM Studios:

> According to plans for the theme park announced recently, the movie *Who Framed Roger Rabbit?* made by a Disney subsidiary, Touchstone Pictures, will serve as the source for an area called Roger Rabbit's Hollywood [to] be built in the mid-1990s. This will be a kind of Toontown, where—as in the movie—only cartoon characters may live. Visitors will meet the movie's eponymous cartoon hero, ride a Toontown trolley rocked by flight simulators, hop into Benny the cartoon cab, and careen in oversized Baby Herman's baby buggy through a Toontown hospital.

The starring attraction for Roger Rabbit's Hollywood would have been Baby Herman's Runaway Baby Buggy Ride, a dark-ride concept similar to those used in several Fantasyland attractions. The attraction would have drawn inspiration from *Tummy Trouble*, a Roger Rabbit short film created in 1989. While the name doesn't exactly roll off the tongue, the actual attraction would have been an innovative and exciting guest experience.

In both *Who Framed Roger Rabbit?* and *Tummy Trouble*, Baby Herman is featured as the gruff, foul-mouthed, cigar-smoking baby perhaps best known for the quote "the whole thing stinks like yesterday's diapers."

The backstory of the attraction would have guests visiting the fictional Maroon Studios. While standing in line for a tour of the newest Roger Rabbit cartoon, *Tummy Trouble*, guests would pass by the trailer of Baby Herman himself. After Baby Herman refuses to film a dangerous scene, a desperate director enlists the help of guests to fill in for the Toontown star. Guests would then load into their ride vehicles, enormous over-sized baby buggies.

During their journey, guests would have taken a harrowing journey through the interior of Toontown Hospital. In the process, they would go down stairs, make hairpin turns, jump over beds and the patients laying in them, and generally get into the type of crazy hijinks that one would expect in the world of Roger Rabbit.

Disney Imagineers also conceptualized a motion-based simulator attraction known as the Toontown Trolley. Think of this as a wacky version of Star Tours (the existing *Star Wars*-themed simulator attraction in Disney's Hollywood Studios), only with more screens and heavy theming showing the hijinks of Roger himself. One of the more exciting possibilities for this attraction was that Roger was rumored to be the actual "driver" of the Trolley, taking guests on a mad-capped tour of Toontown.

Finally, Disney planned another dark-ride concept known as the Benny the Cab Ride, based on the gruff yellow taxicab of the same name. Guests would have ridden, as you might have guessed, in taxicabs through a series of adventures featuring Roger Rabbit, Jessica Rabbit, and the notorious weasels.

In addition to this wide range of attraction offerings, Roger Rabbit's Hollywood would have also featured an authentic re-creation of the Terminal Bar from the film, complete with appearances by numerous "toons" that would have provided the area with a fun dining location.

Plans for Roger Rabbit's Hollywood progressed to the point where Disney advertised the coming land in a variety of marketing materials. In 1991, Disney aired *Walt Disney World Past, Present and Future*, a television tribute in celebration of Walt Disney World's twentieth birthday. In that show, actor John Lithgow references a variety of projects currently underway in Disney World. He specifically mentions Sunset Boulevard, then under construction, and noted that "you'll be able to take a wild trip on the Toontown Transit, a runway bus that hurdles through the cartoon streets of Toontown."

## Egos, *Dick Tracy*, and *Arachnophobia*

Despite the clear connection between Disney's Hollywood Studios and *Who Framed Roger Rabbit?*, and despite the promising initial plans created by Imagineers, Roger Rabbit's Hollywood never came to be. The ultimate reason for that failure most likely originated with a disagreement between Disney and Michael Eisner on one side and Amblin Entertainment and Steven Spielberg on the other.

Following the enormous success of *Who Framed Roger Rabbit?*, rumors of a sequel began almost immediately. While those rumors unfortunately never resulted in an actual full-length feature film, three short films based on the Roger Rabbit characters were developed. The first, *Tummy Trouble*, was released as an introductory short for the 1989 Disney live-action film *Honey, I Shrunk the Kids*. The success of *Tummy Trouble* was credited with having a significant positive impact on the box office revenues of *Honey, I Shrunk the Kids*.

Disney and Amblin developed a second theatrical short entitled *Roller Coaster Rabbit*. Based on the success of *Tummy Trouble*, and the corresponding increase in box office sales for *Honey, I Shrunk the Kids*, both Disney and Spielberg had eyes on the second Roger Rabbit short to push two different feature films. Although it now seems like an odd combination, Spielberg wanted *Roller Coaster Rabbit* to be released with *Arachnophobia* (1990), a spine-chilling thriller based on deadly spiders. Arachnophobia was, not surprisingly, an Amblin Entertainment film. Disney, on the other hand, wanted *Roller Coaster Rabbit* released with its newest live-action film for which it had expended substantial capital, *Dick Tracy* (1990).

Ultimately, *Roller Coaster Rabbit* was released with *Dick Tracy*. This move created an enormous rift between Amblin and Disney and, more specifically, Spielberg and Eisner. Although a third Roger Rabbit short film, *Trail Mix-Up*, was created and released with the 1993 Disney film *A Far Off Place*, the fractured relationship between Disney and Amblin was never the same. For purposes of Roger Rabbit's Hollywood, this created a significant problem because the approval of both Amblin and Disney was needed in order to move the project forward. Although there is no definitive answer as to why plans for Roger Rabbit's Hollywood were ultimately scrapped, one can only imagine that the creative disagreement between Eisner and Spielberg played a significant role.

Despite these disagreements, it still might seem strange that Disney would walk away from an intellectual property franchise that was such a perfect thematic fit for its new park and almost guaranteed to generate significant revenues. One can only imagine that the massive success of the Disney animated films that followed *Who Framed Roger Rabbit?* played a large part in this decision. A potentially long, drawn-out, and expensive legal battle with Amblin and Spielberg probably seemed unnecessary now that the Disney animation renaissance was well underway, with a wide variety of films and characters available for Disney Imagineers to use that would not require any profit sharing with Amblin Entrainment. As a result, what had seemed only months before like such a sure-fire concept for Walt Disney World evaporated altogether (although no "dip" was involved).

## Finding Roger Rabbit in Walt Disney World: Yesterday and Today

One of the bigger misconceptions is that Roger Rabbit was never represented to any significant degree in the Disney World theme parks. Nothing could be further from the truth. First and foremost, a walk around Roger Rabbit character complete with red overhauls, blue eyes, and red hair roamed the streets of the Disney-MGM Studios soon after that park opened.

The Studio Backlot Tour was an opening day attraction for Disney-MGM Studios. It provided a combination tram and walking tour of the backlot areas of the park giving guests a behind-the-scenes look at a working film studio. At the end of the tour, guests could follow outlines of Roger Rabbit's footprints into an area known as the Looney Bin. The Looney Bin was part of an ACME Warehouse, which was a prominent company brand in the Roger Rabbit film. The location served as a unique souvenir shop with numerous photo opportunity pieces and unique movie props from the film, most notably the Dip Mobile and the large steamroller vehicle that killed Judge Doom. The steamroller in particular provided guests with the opportunity to get fantastic photos, mimicking the disastrous fate of Judge Doom. Another fun prop in the Looney Bin was the proverbial "ton of bricks" hanging from the ceiling, as well as a variety of "ACME" boxes and bombs scattered throughout the area. Perhaps the most popular aspect of the Loony Bin was that guests could take a picture with a life-size silhouette of the cartoonishly seductive Jessica Rabbit alongside a cutout of Roger going through a brick wall. The Studio Backlot Tour closed in 2014 to make way for *Star Wars*- and Pixar-themed expansions to the park.

The Monster Sound Show was another opening day experience available to guests on May 1, 1989. Guests could be selected to help record sound effects for a short comedy featuring Martin Short and Chevy Chase. The Monster Sound Show also offered a post-show area known as Soundworks, where guests were able to experiment with sound effects in a hands-on environment. For a time, guests could try their best Roger Rabbit impersonation there.

Roger Rabbit was also included in several parades in the Magic Kingdom. Roger was the grand marshal for Walt Disney World's 20th Anniversary Surprise Celebration that began in 1991. He also temporarily made an appearance as the conductor of a musical float in the Spectromagic Parade, but was replaced by another popular character from the Disney animation renaissance, the Genie from the 1992 film *Aladdin*. In addition, Roger was featured in numerous other stage shows and character interaction experiences throughout the Disney parks.

At Pleasure Island (now a part of Disney Springs), a Jessica's of Hollywood store based on the seductive character of Roger Rabbit's wife, Jessica Rabbit, was open for a period of time. It was a lingerie store that mimicked the famous Fredericks of Hollywood store, and featured a large sign of Jessica that would seductively cross her legs. Jessica's of Hollywood has long since closed.

While the above examples of Roger Rabbit experiences have long since disappeared from Walt Disney World, guests can still find numerous tributes to the film in several areas of Hollywood Studios. The first and most obvious such tribute is a large billboard for Maroon Studios, the fictional production company in *Who Framed Roger Rabbit?* The sign features large portraits of Roger Rabbit, Baby Herman, and Jessica Rabbit. The billboard is a beautiful display, although the colors used thereon have clearly faded from their original glory. It can be found to the left of Hollywood Boulevard in the Echo Lake area.

Another tribute to *Who Framed Roger Rabbit?* can also be found in the Echo Lake area on a series of second-story windows above the Hollywood and Vine restaurant. One window includes the inscription "Eddie Valiant. Private Investigations. All Crime. Surveillance. Missing Person." The next window has a silhouette of Roger Rabbit himself as though the exuberant bunny has been literally thrown out of the building. These windows pay tribute to investigator Eddie Valiant from the film and also replicate a famous scene where Roger blasts through the window after finding out that his dear wife Jessica may have had an affair—by playing patty-cake.

On the opening day for Disney-MGM Studios, in the entrance courtyard to The Great Movie Ride, Roger Rabbit (along with numerous other celebrities) imprinted his hand and footprints into the wet concrete. Roger's square is located near the very center of the courtyard. The celebrity tribute includes an inscription that reads "PL-L-L-Leese. Roger Rabbit. May 1, 1989."

The Backlot Express in Hollywood Studios is a counter service dining location near the Star Tours attraction in the Echo Lake area. The restaurant is themed as a working film backstage area with paint, supplies, models, and props all used to provide theming for the restaurant. At the Backlot Express, guests can see a stripped-down vehicle that was used to film the Benny the Cab sequence from *Who Framed Roger Rabbit?* It is not the finished product that guests viewed on screen, looking more instead like a primitive golf cart. But the prop features the actual seat that actor Bob Hoskins sat on for the filming while the cartoon cab was drawn around him. There are also a variety of photos displayed around the vehicle showing scenes from the film and other behind-the-scenes moments. For a time, the Toon Patrol car driven by Judge Doom's henchmen, the weasels, was also on display as a photo opportunity for guests at the Backlot Express.

Stepping outside of Hollywood Studios, guests can also find Roger Rabbit in the Disney resort hotels. Specifically, in the 1980s section of Disney's Pop Century Resort, guests can see a large statute of Roger standing on a barrel of turpentine that is, appropriately, turned over.

While Hollywood Studios never received a Benny the Cab dark ride, both Disneyland and Tokyo Disneyland got Roger Rabbit's Car Toon Spin, dark ride attractions that essentially replicated the Benny the Cab ride conceptual plans. The Disneyland version opened in January 1994, and the Tokyo Disneyland version opened in April 1996. In the California and Tokyo versions, guests take a ride with Lenny the Cab, Benny's brother. This play on names was no doubt a result of the long-standing disagreement between Disney and Amblin over use of the Roger Rabbit characters.

CHAPTER ELEVEN

# Mickey's Movieland

*During the last few years, we've ventured into a lot of different fields. We've had the opportunity to meet and work with a lot of wonderful people. I only hope we never lose sight of one thing—that it was all started by a Mouse.*

— Walt Disney

The Walt Disney Company has entertained fans for almost a century through numerous heartwarming, lovable, funny, and compelling stories told through a variety of different media, including both television and film. During this time, Disney has created hundreds of lovable characters that inspire happiness, wonder, and hope for generations of fans, many of which remain popular despite being decades old. A few of my personal favorites are Peter Pan from the 1953 film of the same name, Ichabod Crane from the 1949 package film *The Adventures of Ichabod and Mr. Toad*, and Woody and Buzz Lightyear from the *Toy Story* film franchise. Notwithstanding an impressive library of characters that spans over nine decades, no other character is more symbolic of Disney or more beloved by legions of fans than Mickey Mouse. No other character is more closely associated with a particular business than Mickey is with the Disney company.

Mickey Mouse's first noteworthy appearance on film came in 1928 as part of the classic short film *Steamboat Willie*. Since that time, Mickey has appeared in hundreds of television shows, full-length feature films, and short films. Because the legacy of Mickey Mouse started with a short film, it only made sense for Mickey to be featured in Disney's third major theme park that celebrates both feature films and television, Disney-MGM Studios (now Disney's Hollywood Studios).

## A Home For Mickey in the Studios?

When Disney-MGM Studios opened on May 1, 1989, the park's feature attraction was The Great Movie Ride. In this attraction, which continues to entertain visitors today, guests travel through famous scenes from a number of notable films across a variety of genres. Each scene features audio-animatronic characters portraying famous actors and actresses. The films represented are *Footlight Parade* (1933), *Singin' in the Rain* (1952), *Mary Poppins* (1964), *The Public Enemy* (1931), *A Fistful of Dollars* (1964), *The Searchers* (1956), *Alien* (1979), *Raiders of the Lost Ark* (1981), *Tarzan the Ape Man* (1932), *Casablanca* (1942), and *The Wizard of Oz* (1939). Given the significance of Mickey Mouse's character to the entire Disney organization, it made sense to have Mickey featured to some extent in The Great Movie Ride. Although he did not get a stand-alone scene featuring audio-animatronic characters like the above referenced films, Mickey is featured briefly in a projection from the 1940 animated film *Fantasia*.

Disney executives originally thought that Disney-MGM Studios would only be a half-day park. However, the park instantly become popular with guests, and so Disney almost immediately began plans to expand it. These plans ultimately resulted in the addition of a new street, Sunset Boulevard. As part of this expansion, Imagineers saw an opportunity to significantly increase Mickey Mouse's presence in the park, while at the same time paying tribute to the earliest years of Disney animation.

## A Replica of Hyperion Avenue Studios

One of the attraction concepts proposed for Sunset Boulevard was Mickey's Movieland, a concept previously intended for an "Entertainment Pavilion" in Epcot. While plans for this experience morphed and evolved over time, we know that Mickey's Movieland would tell the history of filmmaking, with an emphasis on Mickey Mouse himself. It was to have an attraction featuring audio-animatronic characters and vintage clips from Mickey Mouse classic movies and short films. The plans also included a number of exhibits featuring vintage animation equipment and a number of displays on the history and process of animation. The result would have been a quasi-animation museum in which guests would learn various aspects of the movie making industry.

The exterior façade of Mickey's Movieland would have been amazing, especially for fans of early Disney animation. Specifically, the show building for Mickey's Movieland would have re-created the movie studio used by the Disney company from 1926 until 1940, at 2719 Hyperion Avenue, Los Angeles, California.

The Hyperion Avenue studio was significant for a number of reasons, not least because it was Walt and Roy Disney's first real studio. Before Hyperion, the brothers literally worked out of a garage, moving later into the back of a real estate agency to produce their early animation works.

The Hyperion Avenue studio is also where Walt developed Mickey Mouse, the character that would become synonymous with Walt and the Disney company as a whole. The show building for Mickey's Movieland would have been enormous, a full-scale re-creation of the Hyperion Avenue studio.

From a thematic standpoint, Mickey's Movieland was a perfect fit for Disney-MGM Studios. The time period of the late 1920s and 1930s tied in well with the era of Hollywood depicted there. For a park dedicated to film, television, and radio, a replica of the famous Disney studio was a match made in heaven.

Despite the natural fit, Mickey's Movieland never came to be. The reason why is not clear. Ultimately, the idea of a nostalgic and educational playground was replaced with another starring attraction: The Twilight Zone Tower of Terror, a more adult-focused, adrenaline-pumping experience, which opened on July 22, 1994.

## Finding Mickey's Movieland in Walt Disney World Today

While plans for Mickey's Movieland never materialized, several of its key components were incorporated into other guest experiences. For example, the process of creating cartoons, which would have been a prominent part of Mickey's Movieland, was a central feature of the Magic of Disney Animation, a combination tour and guest experience that ran from the park's opening day on May 1, 1989, until July 12, 2015.

Other exhibits and displays intended for Mickey's Movieland also ended up in Hollywood Studios. For example, the revolutionary multiplane camera invented by Walt Disney was placed in Walt Disney: One Man's Dream, a walk-through tribute to Walt Disney that opened in October 2001. Given the number of wholesale changes currently taking place at Hollywood Studios, it remains to be seen whether Walt Disney: One Man's Dream will survive or, as some have suggested, be removed altogether in favor of the massive Toy Story Land additions that are coming to the park.

## CHAPTER TWELVE

# Dick Tracy's Crime Stoppers

*All right, that's enough! I want 'em dead, both of 'em. I want this no-face character dead and I want Tracy dead. What's the matter, you bums forgot how to kill people? Doesn't your work mean anything to you anymore? Have you no sense of pride in what you do? No sense of duty, no sense of destiny? I'm looking for generals, what do I got? Foot soldiers! I want Dick Tracy DEAD!*

— Big Boy Caprice, *Dick Tracy* (1990)

Disney knows exactly what to do with blockbuster feature films. It rolls out a wide variety of merchandise featuring the characters from the film, incorporates them into theme park attractions, and in some cases even completely separate theme park lands, makes sequels and spinoffs, and, most importantly for the corporate bottom line, earns a whole lot of money. For example, in 2003 Disney released *Pirates of the Caribbean*, loosely based on the Disneyland and Walt Disney World attractions of the same name. Following the overwhelming success of that film, Disney Imagineers made additions and changes to each of the theme park attractions to incorporate aspects from the film. They also rolled out shirts, hats, toys, and books with Jack Sparrow and the other characters from the movie, and released three sequels (with a fourth sequel expected to be released in 2017). This same pattern is playing out today with the massive success of the 2013 animated film *Frozen*, Disney's newly acquired rights to the *Star Wars* franchise of films, and numerous Pixar franchises, such as *Toy Story* and *Cars*.

In 1990, Disney believed that it had just such a blockbuster in production. *Dick Tracy* had everything: a charismatic hero, a variety of dastardly villains, a pair of beautiful leading ladies, an intriguing setting in 1930s gangster-era Chicago, and an all-star cast. Disney believed that *Dick Tracy* would be a tremendous box-office success and the beginning of a franchise that would result in numerous merchandising opportunities and theme park attractions and experiences. As a result, the company placed enormous expectations on the film that only a comic-book hero could reach. Unfortunately for Disney, that comic-book hero was not a police investigator from Chicago, but instead a bat from Gotham.

## Dick Tracy

The character of Dick Tracy has been represented in variety of comic books, magazines, radio shows, movies, and television serials dating back to the 1930s. In the late 1980s, Jeffrey Katzenberg, the head of the animation and motion picture groups of the Disney company, brokered a deal with Warren Beatty to put a long-contemplated Dick Tracy film into production. Beatty had been trying to make a Tracy film for almost twenty years, but after a series of cancellations and delays across various movie studios, the project was finally ready to become a reality.

*Dick Tracy* is set in an exaggerated version of 1930s Chicago at the height of the gangster era. Pursuant to Beatty's insistence, the film's look and feel represents the comic book origins of Dick Tracy, and seems in many respects cartoonish in nature. The story revolves around the struggles of Dick Tracy, a police detective with high intelligence, quick fists, and a signature yellow overcoat and fedora, to combat criminal activity throughout Chicago. At the heart of those struggles are Big Boy Caprice, the notorious crime boss of Chicago, and his numerous henchmen. Along the way, viewers are introduced to the seductive and mysterious Breathless Mahoney, the sole witness to a number of Big Boy Caprice crimes; Tess Trueheart, Dick Tracy's girlfriend; and the Kid, an orphan living on the streets of Chicago who is taken in by Tracy.

Beatty of *Bonnie and Clyde* (1967) and *Heaven Can Wait* (1978) fame played Dick Tracy, while Al Pacino, whose numerous starring roles included *The Godfather* (1972) and *Scarface* (1983), portrayed Big Boy Caprice. Perhaps the most controversial and criticized casting decision for the film was the choice of Madonna to play the role of Breathless Mahoney. Other notable actors featured in *Dick Tracy* were Dustin Hoffman and William Forsythe as Caprice henchmen; James Caan as Spud Spaldoni, a secondary crime boss; and Dick Van Dyke as District Attorney John Fletcher.

## A Dick Tracy Presence in the Studios

When Disney-MGM Studios opened on May 1, 1989, it became an instant success. Disney executives and Imagineers soon worked on options to expand the park and add a full complement of attractions and experiences. One leading candidate was an attraction based on the soon-to-be released film *Dick Tracy*. Plans for this attraction, known as Dick Tracy's Crime Stoppers, contemplated an entirely separate area surrounding the attraction themed to the world of Dick Tracy, complete with vintage industrial Chicago cityscapes and buildings from the film, as well as a variety of shops and other experiences for guests.

As Disney expected the film to be a blockbuster, it also felt that the franchise needed a likewise blockbuster theme park attraction. Disney Imagineers had worked tirelessly on developing a new ride vehicle technology known as an Enhanced Motion Vehicle or EMV. An EMV is essentially a motion simulator on wheels. By using a complex system of hydraulic pumps, the ride vehicles can simulate driving over extremely hilly or rough terrains, even though the actual surface upon which the vehicle is travelling is completely flat.

Dick Tracy's Crime Stoppers was to be the first Disney theme park attraction that used EMV technology. The attraction would replicate an exaggerated and fictional depiction of the 1930s. However, instead of the glitz and glamour of Golden Age Hollywood, Dick Tracy's Crime Stoppers would focus on the classic gangster era of 1930s Chicago, complete with abandoned warehouses, dark alleys, and numerous fictionalized gangsters. Imagineers created several conceptual drawings that predominately focused on the general setting of the proposed attraction as opposed to ride specifics. These drawings depict an area set in perpetual darkness, with low-lit streets hiding mysteries around every corner and potential trouble down every alley.

In Crime Stoppers, the Enhanced Motion Vehicles would take guests through 1930s Chicago down grimy streets, through industrial warehouses, and past the Chicago docks while chasing a variety of notorious comic-book gangsters. During the experience, bullets would be fired from all sides with interactive elements such as the sound of breaking glass adding authenticity to the experience. Guests would be armed with tommy guns to battle the gangsters encountered during the exciting chase. These guns would have been similar to those later used in Buzz Lightyear's Space Ranger Spin in the Magic Kingdom.

## High Expectations and Legal Battles

The Disney company placed enormous expectations on *Dick Tracy*. In its 1989 Annual Report, Disney executives emphasized that "[t]he film's potential is tremendous as theatrical entertainment and as a catalyst for merchandising and spin-off benefits for the entire company."

From a critical standpoint, *Dick Tracy* won three Academy Awards for Best Art Direction, Best Makeup, and Best Original Song for "Sooner or

Later (I Always Get My Man)," as well as numerous other nominations, including a Best Supporting Actor nomination for Al Pacino.

One of the bigger misconceptions in Disney circles is that *Dick Tracy* was a box-office flop and lost the company millions of dollars. Although the film cost approximately $101 million to make, it grossed approximately $162 million worldwide. Therefore, from a purely financial standpoint, *Dick Tracy* was a commercial success. The reality, however, was that *Dick Tracy* did not even make it into the top five highest grossing films of that year. In fact, it came in at number nine behind *Home Alone*, *Ghost*, *Dances With Wolves*, *Pretty Woman*, *Teenage Mutant Ninja Turtles*, *The Hunt For Red October*, *Total Recall*, and *Die Hard 2* (it was certainly a good year for movies).

Disney's disappointment with *Dick Tracy* had more to do with a blockbuster film from 1989 than with more profitable films from 1990. Jeffrey Katzenberg in particular believed that *Dick Tracy* would match the extremely high bar set by *Batman* (1989) starring Michael Keaton and Jack Nicholson that grossed more than $400 million worldwide and, more importantly, spawned numerous sequels and an enormous amount of merchandising opportunities. But *Dick Tracy* fell far short of the standard set by the Caped Crusader.

Less-than-expected box office numbers were only the beginning of the problems faced by the Disney company in the months following the release of *Dick Tracy*. A significant legal dispute soon developed between Tribune Media Services and Warren Beatty over ownership of the Dick Tracy intellectual property rights and division of profits related to the franchise, which Beatty eventually won many years later. However, the combination of box-office disappointment and ominous legal clouds was all the reason that Disney needed to cancel plans for rolling out the Enhanced Motion Vehicle technology (along with its correspondingly high price tag) on Dick Tracy's Crime Stoppers, and Disney shelved the attraction.

## Here Comes Dick Tracy

Although Dick Tracy's Crime Stoppers never made it into Disney-MGM Studios, the yellow-clad investigator did appear in the park as part of the Dick Tracy Diamond Double-Cross, an outdoor stage show featuring Dick Tracy and other characters from the film. The show took place in the original Theatre of the Stars, which was later removed to make way for Sunset Boulevard. The Dick Tracy Diamond Double-Cross ran for less than a year before being replaced by Beauty and the Beast—Live on Stage.

Walt Disney World did eventually offer an attraction using the Enhanced Motion Vehicle Technology when Countdown to Extinction opened in the DinoLand, U.S.A. section of Animal Kingdom on April 22, 1998. That attraction, later renamed to DINOSAUR, takes guests on a prehistoric journey to the Cretaceous period, with the ride vehicle providing bumps, jolts, and hair-raising action. Countdown to Extinction, however, was not the first Disney attraction to use Enhanced Motion Vehicles. That distinction goes to Temple of the Forbidden Eye (now known as the Indiana Jones Adventure), which opened in Disneyland in 1995.

Although Disney World guests can't fire tommy guns at gangsters in the streets of Chicago, they can fire laser cannons while seated in an XP-37 space cruiser in Buzz Lightyear's Space Ranger Spin. This Tomorrowland attraction opened in 1998 and takes guests through a variety of interactive scenes where they can win points by firing lasers at different targets, all in the name of saving the universe from the Evil Emperor Zurg.

For guests craving a journey through the gangster era of the 1930s, Hollywood Studios does have The Great Movie Ride, which opened with the rest of the park on May 1, 1989. This attraction features a classic gangster scene set in the smoky back alleys of 1930s Chicago, the same time period and geographic location represented in *Dick Tracy*. Although there are no specific *Dick Tracy* references, guests do see an audio-animatronic James Cagney from the 1931 classic gangster film *The Public Enemy*.

CHAPTER THIRTEEN

# Muppet Studios

*Statler: Hey, Waldorf, what is this anyway?*
*Waldorf: Oh, it's one of those 3-D movies. Better put on your glasses.*
*[Statler does so]*
*Statler: [looking at the audience] Hey, check out the guy in the Goofy mask.*
*Waldorf: That's no mask.*
*Statler: Ooops. Sorry, lady!*

— Statler and Waldorf, Muppet*Vision 3D

The quote is from one of my favorite attractions in all of Walt Disney World, Muppet*Vision 3D. This theatre show opened on May 16, 1991, in the Streets of America section of Disney-MGM Studios. It combines a zany queue, a funny pre-show movie, a 3D film, hilarious audio-animatronics, bubbles, water, an exploding theater, and even a live-action character to create a fun experience that the entire family can enjoy together. Although Muppet Vision has entertained guests for over twenty years, it looked as though the Muppet era was coming to an end in 2015 when a series of blockbuster announcements were made at the D23 (the "official" Disney fan club) Expo in Anaheim, California, that would change Disney's Hollywood Studios forever.

Disney executives announced that the park would be largely re-themed with the additions of Toy Story Land, an area dedicated to the Pixar animated film franchise of the same name, and, perhaps even more exciting, a new land devoted to the world of *Star Wars*. In order to make room for these additions, numerous attractions and experiences were closed in the months that followed, including the Studio Backlot Tour, the Lights, Motors, Action! Stunt Show, and the Honey, I Shrunk the Kids Movie Set Adventure. Notably, all of these shuttered attractions surround Muppet*Vision 3D, leading many to believe that it would also be on the chopping block.

Disney surprised many by not only keeping Muppet*Vision 3D, but also announcing an expansion of the Muppet presence in the park with the addition of a Muppet-themed restaurant. While Muppet fans around the world rejoiced at this decision, few realize that, twenty years prior to this announcement, Disney Imagineers had developed plans for a completely separate theme park land known as Muppet Studios. This land would not only have included a 3D show and a Muppet restaurant, but also a marquee headliner attraction known as the Great Muppet Movie Ride. So why did Muppet Studios and its headliner attraction never come to be? Unfortunately, the answer to that question begins with the tragic death of the brilliant artist and puppeteer behind the Muppets, Jim Henson.

## Muppet Studios

As was the case with the concepts for Roger Rabbit's Hollywood and Dick Tracy's Crime Stoppers, Imagineers developed plans for Muppet Studios in response to the overwhelming success of Disney-MGM Studios and the need to quickly add attractions to deal with guest capacity issues. One of their ideas was a separate theme park area devoted to the Muppets.

Muppet Studios would have included a variety of zany, comical, slapstick attractions and experiences featuring Kermit the Frog, Miss Piggy, and the rest of the Muppet crew. The Great Muppet Movie Ride was to be the headliner attraction, and one on which Disney was to spare no expense.

The Great Muppet Movie Ride would have been a parody of The Great Movie Ride, the marquee attraction that salutes the genre of feature films and takes guests through scenes from numerous classic movies. The Muppet version would have also taken guests through a variety of scenes from classic films. The difference, however, would be that these otherwise famous movie scenes would be re-created with Muppet characters.

Disney advertised that the Great Muppet Movie Ride would be a "misguided tour through movie history." In a promotional video segment entitled "Dateline Walt Disney World" created by Disney about a variety of upcoming attractions for Disney-MGM Studios, an exuberant Jim Henson describes the attraction as "a backstage ride explaining how movies are shot...but all the information is wrong."

Two pieces of conceptual artwork for the Great Muppet Movie Ride depict a pair of these comical scenes. The first is a hilarious depiction of the 1931 classic monster film *Frankenstein*, with Muppet characters filling in for the live actors in the scene. The role of Frankenstein is played by a very large and very distraught Beaker, who is strapped down in a tube as Dr. Bunsen Honeydew (standing in for Dr. Victor Frankenstein) performs a variety of experiments. Gonzo is directing the scene, and Rizzo the Rat and several of his friends provide the electricity needed for the experiment via a hamster wheel. Also featured is Fozzie Bear, who holds a wire in each hand and receives a large jolt of the Rizzo-created electricity.

Another conceptual drawing depicts a Muppet version of the 1953 Disney animated film *Peter Pan*. Specifically, the artwork depicts the famous scene of Peter Pan, Tinker Bell, and the Darling children flying over London. Kermit the Frog stars as Peter Pan, and Miss Piggy plays Tinker Bell. A number of "backstage" Muppets are shown struggling to help Miss Piggy "fly." The filming takes a disastrous turn, with Miss Piggy crashing to the ground while the entire set is in disarray. Gonzo is again directing (although with much less success this time around), while Fozzie Bear, Skeeter, and Janice play the roles of John, Michael, and Wendy Darling.

A pair of old Muppet curmudgeons, Statler and Waldorf, would offer perhaps the best comic relief in the Great Muppet Movie Ride by adding their signature brand of sarcastic humor to each attraction scene.

In addition to the Great Muppet Movie Ride, Muppet Studios would have also included two experiences that are no doubt familiar with guests today. The first, a theatre show called Muppet*Vision 3D, opened on May 16, 1991. The second, a restaurant known as The Great Gonzo's Pandemonium Pizza Parlor, would have provided Muppet grub for guests visiting Muppet Studios. This establishment would have been a combination pizza restaurant and Muppet museum, with a variety of Muppet mementos scattered throughout the restaurant similar to the Planet Hollywood restaurant franchise. The backstory was that Gonzo had partnered with Rizzo the Rat to create a pizza restaurant. And who better to hire to actually bake the pizzas than the crazy Swedish Chef.

## Muppet Negotiations and Tragedy

The Muppets are the creation of artist and puppeteer Jim Henson. Henson's credits include his early work on the children's program *Sesame Street* and amazing puppet work on projects such as *Fraggle Rock*, a live-action puppet television program for children that first aired in the early 1980s, and the 1982 film *The Dark Crystal*. However, Henson is most famous for creating the Muppets, a term that collectively refers to a wide variety of puppet characters including Kermit the Frog, Miss Piggy, Fozzie Bear, and Gonzo. The Muppets have been featured in numerous movies, television series, books, and magazines over a period of more than fifty years.

The connection between Disney and Henson was a natural one. Henson's imagination, creativity, and focus on family-friendly entertainment was cut from the same cloth as that of Disney's creative leaders. In *The Imagineering Field Guide to Disney's Hollywood Studios at Walt Disney World* (2010), this connection is described in relation to the Muppet*Vision 3D attraction:

> [Muppet*Vision 3D] was a further attempt to reach beyond the universe of Disney film, television, and character properties in the Park, using the Muppet world created by Jim Henson—which was chosen because it was such a strong companion to the Disney canon. Jim Henson's commitment to character development and maintaining an internal integrity to the stories being told was very much in alignment with Walt Disney's.

In the late 1980s, the Disney company actively negotiated a deal with Henson that would have provided for Disney's acquisition of the Muppet franchise. Henson would have remained a consultant and actively involved on Disney's future Muppet projects. By all accounts, these negotiations were going very well and completion of the deal was imminent. Michael Eisner even made an announcement in his letter to shareholders that accompanied the 1989 Annual Report of The Walt Disney Company:

> In our most recent acquisition, we expect to finalize our purchase of Henson Associates, Inc. soon, including its popular film and television library and more than 40 of his famous Muppet characters led by Kermit the Frog. We expect Jim [Henson], his unbelievable talent and existing properties to be major contributors starting this coming year and through the decade.

Things were going so well that Henson was already working on several Muppet projects with Disney, including Muppet*Vision 3D. Unfortunately, Henson passed away on May 16, 1990, at the age of fifty-three. The film and television community around the world mourned this tragic loss. Disney announced that Henson "was a friend, a colleague, a soft-spoken genius and a television visionary" and that "[t]he world is indeed a poorer place with his passing." Muppet*Vision 3D was Henson's last major project, with the attraction opening exactly one year following his death.

Although the business negotiations between Disney and Henson were almost complete, the parties had not yet signed the appropriate legal documents to close the deal. There are numerous rumors about why the Muppet acquisition stalled after Henson's death, including that his heirs were offended when Disney pushed forward with negotiating the deal without allowing them time to grieve. Regardless of the reason, Disney was not able to acquire the Muppets outright in the 1990s (that transaction would not take place until more than a decade later, in 2005). Instead, Disney would only be able to license Muppet characters for specific attractions and experiences. While Disney was able to negotiate deals to use the characters in Muppet*Vision 3D, a parade, and a stage show, no such deal was reached for the Great Muppet Movie Ride or the other proposed concepts for Muppet Studios.

## Finding the Muppets Today

The good news for Muppet fans is that Kermit the Frog, Miss Piggy, Gonzo, Fozzie Bear, Sam Eagle, and the other Muppet characters can be found throughout Disney World today, in particular at Muppet*Vision 3D in Disney's Hollywood Studios. Once guests exit that attraction, they can also get their Muppet-merchandise fix at the adjacent Stage One Company Store. Stage One offers a variety of Muppet-themed items ranging from shirts and caps to plushes and figurines. It is themed as the set of the Happiness Hotel from the 1981 film *The Great Muppet Caper.*

Although The Great Gonzo's Pandemonium Pizza Parlor never made it off of the drawing boards and into the parks, a similar concept, The Famous Original PizzeRizzo, is set to open in late 2016 in the building formerly occupied by Toy Story Pizza Planet. As the name indicates, this restaurant is "owned" by Rizzo the Rat, the street-smart and wisecracking rodent from the Muppet films and television series. Disney describes the establishment as follows:

> Walt Disney Imagineering hid hints of Rizzo, his extended family and friends who have visited PizzeRizzo over the years throughout the two-story quick-service location. In addition to the expansive indoor and outdoor seating area, guests will be able to dine in a "'cheesy" banquet room, or take five in a special booth designated just for Rizzo's celebrity friends.

Not wanting to leave Gonzo out of the fun, Disney renamed the restrooms adjacent to the Original PizzeRizzo as Gonzo's Royal Flush.

The Muppets also ventured into Liberty Square in the Magic Kingdom in 2016 with The Muppets Present...Great Moments in American History, which Disney describes as:

> Sam Eagle, the fiercely patriotic American eagle who is forever trying to set a high moral standard for the Muppets, will join Kermit the Frog, Miss Piggy, Fozzie Bear, The Great Gonzo and James Jefferson, town crier of Liberty Square, as they gather outside The Hall of Presidents to present historical tales in hysterical fashion as only they can. From the midnight ride of Paul Revere to the signing of the Declaration of Independence, the Muppets appear throughout the day to share with Guests their own unique take on the founding fathers and the birth of the United States of America.

In the words of Sam Eagle, anyone who doesn't enjoy the Muppets in Walt Disney World is "distinctly unpatriotic."

CHAPTER FOURTEEN

# David Copperfield's Magic Underground

*I try to help people realize their dreams by using magic to tell stories that educate, move, and inspire.*

— David Copperfield

Theme park lands and attractions are not the only things that Disney Imagineers painstakingly plan, design, and theme. Walt Disney World is also home to a wide variety of intricately detailed restaurants that are much more than simply places to grab a good meal. Many of these restaurants are fantastic experiences in and of themselves that, like so many other things in the Disney parks, immerse guests in an entertaining story. For example, the 50's Prime Time Café in Disney's Hollywood Studios is themed as your mom's kitchen straight out of the 1950s. This theme is carried out to perfection through the use of vintage props and chatty cast members who will remind guests to finish their vegetables and to take their elbows off the table. Guests can also dine at the Be Our Guest Restaurant in the Magic Kingdom, set within the grand halls of Beast's castle from the classic 1991 Disney animated feature film *Beauty and the Beast*, complete with massive chandeliers and simulated snow falling through dramatic floor-to-ceiling windows.

In 1996, Disney announced plans for another highly themed restaurant that would have been unlike anything in Disney World at that time. Known as the Copperfield Magic Underground, this restaurant would have been made in partnership with famed magician David Copperfield. The Magic Underground would have included props from Copperfield's many impressive magical performances as well as illusions and magic tricks performed directly in front of guests as they dined. Unfortunately, plans for the Magic Underground "disappeared" due to very un-magical reasons—namely, Copperfield's own extremely high standards and even higher cost overruns.

## David Copperfield

David Copperfield is one of the world's most popular and commercially successful magicians. His most notable accomplishments include making the Statue of Liberty disappear in 1983 and walking through the Great Wall of China in 1986. Copperfield has received twenty-one Emmy Awards, a star on the Hollywood Walk of Fame, and holds numerous Guinness world records. In April 2000, Copperfield received the prestigious Living Legend designation from the Library of Congress.

While Copperfield's career has spanned over forty years, he reached the height of his popularity in the 1980s and the 1990s. During this time, he starred in numerous television specials and headlined thousands of performances around the globe. Copperfield was not only the most popular magician on the planet, but also one of the most popular entertainers as well.

In 1995, entrepreneur and venture capitalist Glen Tullman approached Copperfield about a potential business opportunity. Tullman wanted to capitalize on Copperfield's immense popularity by creating a franchise of highly themed restaurants featuring Copperfield's name and a variety of magical props and tricks. Tullman teamed with Conseco, a large Indiana insurance company, to pull together the needed capital to fund the project. Tullman, Conseco, and Copperfield formed a company named Latenite Magic to move the project forward.

Tullman anticipated that the Magic Underground would become a franchise of restaurants across the county. During this time period, restaurant chains such as Planet Hollywood and the Hard Rock Café were at the peak of their popularity, and the Magic Underground seemed like the perfect opportunity to capitalize on Copperfield's fame. Instead of including memorabilia from famous feature films (like Planet Hollywood) or legendary rock-and-roll bands (like the Hard Rock Café), the Magic Underground would have included a wide array of mementos and noteworthy items from Copperfield's many magical performances, as well as similar items from other famous magicians. The Magic Underground was to be much more than just a restaurant, and was to have been billed as a complete guest experience.

Initial plans for the Magic Underground focused on two locations: New York City and Walt Disney World. The Latenite Magic principals hoped that the Disney relationship would lead to more restaurants in Disney parks in California, Tokyo, and Paris. Latenite Magic initially focused on the New York City location, in Times Square. The Disney company also gave the go-ahead for a Magic Underground in Disney World and a lease was signed for the project.

The Time Square and Disney World versions of the Magic Underground would not have been mirror images of one another. *The New York Times* gave a description of the proposed Times Square restaurant:

> Ultimately, the designs for the Times Square restaurant called for a heroic, 45-foot figure to stand astride the front entrance, flanked by a pair of 18-foot gas torches. Neon signs mounted on the exterior of the building were to erupt every hour in a 90-second light show, with lights proclaiming the site Copperfield's Magic Underground emerging from the display.
>
> Inside, there would be a 70-foot atrium with gargoyles perched on steel trusses in a style [described as] industrial gothic. Diners were to sit on terraces nestled around a model of the Statute of Liberty's torch. To the eye, banquettes and a bar would levitate, while a section of diners would suddenly disappear and, once an hour, the death saw would appear to cut a diner in half. Everywhere, there would be what became known as Davids, large-scale likenesses of Mr. Copperfield.

In Disney World, the Magic Underground would have been located in Disney-MGM Studios, to the right of the park entrance. To maximize visitors, the restaurant would have been accessible by guests without a park admission ticket in much the same way that guests can enter the Rainforest Café at Disney's Animal Kingdom today.

A March 17, 1997, article by Susan Strother in the *Orlando Sentinel* entitled "Customers May Disappear at David Copperfield's Restaurant" described the Disney version of the Magic Underground:

> The Orlando restaurant will have the look of a monument factory that visitors learn is actually Copperfield's workshop. Copperfield will be there daily, sort of, performing magic via video. DAVID, or the Digital Actuating Video Imaging Device, will show Copperfield's face and hands on monitors, on which he'll direct the illusions.

The *Sentinel* article also quotes Copperfield in explaining that the Magic Underground "will be a totally interactive experience. We'll be performing magic. Guests will levitate. People will disappear." The restaurant would have included seating for approximately five hundred guests. Copperfield stated that the Magic Underground's menu would have included "a lot of recipes I have enjoyed during my world tours," including steaks and pizzas.

Disney did not shy away from promoting the Magic Underground, placing multiple billboards in and around the park. These billboards read "COPPERFIELD MAGIC UNDERGROUND" with a "SUMMER 1998" banner in the corner. The billboards even featured a logo for the restaurant that included a torch symbolic of Copperfield's famed Statute of Liberty illusion.

A series of marketing photographs were also taken to promote the Magic Underground. One features Copperfield and then chairman and CEO of the Disney company, Michael Eisner, with Eisner holding a large ring and a set of blueprints labeled "PLANS," "TOP SECRET," "COPPERFIELD," and "MAGIC UNDERGROUND" floating inside the ring.

A second promotional photograph features Sorcerer Mickey Mouse flanked by Copperfield and Judson Green, the president of Disney Attractions in 1996, inside the park. By all accounts, the addition of the Copperfield restaurant to Disney World was a done deal.

## Not-So-Magical Problems

Construction on the Times Square version of the Magic Underground began in 1996. Almost immediately, a rift developed between Copperfield and the other owners of Latenite Magic. One fundamental problem with New York's Magic Underground was that construction began before the conceptual planning and design work were finished. For this and other reasons, numerous design and structural changes pushed the project's cost well beyond its initial projected budget of $20 million. As an extreme example, *New York Times* writer Charles V. Bagli explained that the Magic Underground's signs and the hydraulic systems required for many of the restaurant's illusions "would require the same volume of electrical power as a 40-story skyscraper."

The Times Square location was approximately 85% complete when Latenite Magic ran into more financial problems. One notable factor was that Copperfield did not invest any of his own money in the project. Instead, Copperfield contributed his name to the Magic Underground and retained creative control over the project, notwithstanding his lack of direct financial support. Actual funds for the project came in the form of investment dollars.

Copperfield was a noted perfectionist, insisting that the restaurant's illusions be flawless so as not to damage his reputation. This stood in stark contrast to the other owners of Latenite Magic who simply wanted to get the restaurant opened in order to stop the financial bleeding and to recoup the money already invested. At one point, Tullman even approached a rival magician in an effort to replace Copperfield. Not surprisingly, this move further escalated tensions within the Latenite Magic group.

With costs spiraling out of control and a heated internal struggle being waged between Copperfield and Latenite Magic, work on the Magic Underground in Times Square came to an abrupt stop in January 1998. Soon thereafter, contractors filed a multitude of liens against the property totaling millions of dollars. A September 26, 1999, *New York Times* article entitled "Poof! $34 Million Vanishes on Broadway" stated that, in the months following the stoppage of work in New York, "millions of dollars' worth of illusions for the project are gathering dust in an upstate New York warehouse."

Having witnessed these financial problems and the disastrous end of the Times Square location, the Disney company terminated its lease with Latenite Magic and the billboards advertising the Magic Underground were unceremoniously removed from the parks with no official explanation provided. Just like that, the once-grand plans for the Magic Underground restaurant in Disney World vanished into thin air almost as quickly as the Statute of Liberty had in Copperfield's most famous illusion. Unfortunately for investors in Latenite Magic, approximately $34 million worth of investor funds vanished with it.

## Magical Discoveries in Walt Disney World

Would-be magicians could find a perfect store to meet their magical needs in the Magic Kingdom when the park first opened on October 1, 1971. The House of Magic was a quaint shop located on Main Street, U.S.A. that offered a variety of magic tricks and gags, masks, and puzzles that were pure joy for kids of all ages. The House of Magic was a mainstay on Main Street for almost twenty-five years. In 1995, it was finally closed and replaced by the Main Street Athletic Club, a store specializing in sports-themed merchandise with a Disney twist. The Emporium, the largest shop on Main Street, annexed the location in 2001.

Although Walt Disney World never got a magical restaurant themed on the accomplishments of David Copperfield, it did get a lounge themed as a "magical" watering hole from the 1940s. The AbracadaBar opened on Disney's Boardwalk in 2016, with a detailed backstory:

> Formerly the stomping grounds for famous magicians, local illusionists and the loveliest of magician's assistants, AbracadaBar gives interested onlookers and aficionados of alcoholic beverages alike a glimpse—and perhaps a taste—of another time and place.
>
> According to Boardwalk lore, prestidigitators would gather here after nearly every show, often staying up all night as they attempted to out-charm each other with extraordinary tricks before gathering at the bar to conjure up new cocktails.
>
> But then, just as soon as it had appeared, the secret lounge vanished into thin air, never to be seen again...until today!

The AbracadaBar is richly themed with dark colors and elaborate designs that fit nicely within the 1940s time period represented by the Boardwalk.

The lounge is decorated with numerous magical props, including wands, a straightjacket, and vintage advertisements for fictional magicians such as The Great Nyokaa. For those distraught over the loss of the Copperfield Magic Underground, they can drown those sorrows at the AbracadaBar with magical cocktails such as the Elixir, the Parlor Trick, the Magic Mirror, and the Magic Hattan.

PART FOUR

# Disney's Animal Kingdom

*Welcome to a kingdom of animals...real, ancient and imagined: a kingdom ruled by lions, dinosaurs and dragons; a kingdom of balance, harmony and survival; a kingdom we enter to share in the wonder, gaze at the beauty, thrill at the drama, and learn.*

— Michael D. Eisner, Disney's Animal Kingdom Dedication Plaque

CHAPTER FIFTEEN

# Beastly Kingdom

*If I could pick any job here, I'd move my office to the Imagineering building and immerse myself in all that lunacy and free-thinking.*

— Michael Eisner

Imagine a kingdom based upon myth and legend, a kingdom of good and evil. Imagine a crumbling medieval castle, scorched in flame, home to an enormous fire-breathing dragon guarding a vast treasure. Imagine an elaborate hedge maze, lushly landscaped and filled with mystery and intrigue around every bend. Imagine a land of unicorns, sea monsters, and centaurs. If that sounds to you like a great plan for a theme park, you are not alone.

Beastly Kingdom (also referenced in some materials as Beastlie Kingdomme) was to be an intricately themed land in Disney's Animal Kingdom devoted to creatures of myth, legend, folklore, and fairytales, with a wide variety of fantastic beasts represented therein. Think of it as a Fantasyland for the animal realm. Imagineers were so convinced that Beastly Kingdom would be a runaway hit with guests that they fought for more than a decade to keep the land's construction hopes alive.

So why did this legendary land never come to be? The answer to that question is a wild one, and includes a truth even more unbelievable than the myths upon which Beastly Kingdom would be based: Disney Imagineers were so desperate to build the land that they actually cheered for their most fierce rival in central Florida, Universal Studios, to steal guests away from the Most Magical Place on Earth.

## The Road to Disney's Animal Kingdom

Animal Kingdom officially opened to the public on Earth Day, April 22, 1998. The massive project represented Disney World's fourth major theme park and, at over five hundred acres in size, its largest. Animal Kingdom was also a significant departure from Disney's other parks around the world, as it would be dedicated to animal conservation, education, and entertainment. While the park would have numerous opportunities for guests to observe real wildlife, Disney executives and Imagineers knew from the very beginning that Animal Kingdom would be much more than just a zoological experience.

The Disney company invested countless research and development hours into the Animal Kingdom project. Disney sent Imagineers on numerous trips to Africa and Asia and developed a wide variety of partnerships with zoological and conservation experts and organizations across the world. Based on this research and Disney's ideological goals for the park, the company decided that Animal Kingdom would represent three separate and distinct classifications of animals: real, extinct, and imagined.

The "real" animals in Animal Kingdom would be represented in Africa and Asia, two lushly landscaped lands dedicated to the culture, history, and wildlife of those continents; the Oasis, a rainforest-themed welcome area for the park; and Rafiki's Planet Watch, an area dedicated to animal conservation and education. "Extinct" animals would be represented in DinoLand, U.S.A., a land devoted to dinosaurs. Finally, "imagined" animals from myth and legend would be represented in a land known as Beastly Kingdom.

The proposed Beastly Kingdom section of Animal Kingdom played a large role in the park being developed in the first place. In fact, Beastly Kingdom scored very high in guest surveys about a proposed fourth Disney World theme park, with guests identifying this mythical area as a primary reason to make return visits to a new animal-themed park.

## The Beastly Kingdom Theme and Layout

Thanks to a large number of beautiful conceptual drawings, artwork, and other marketing literature, we understand a great deal about what Beastly Kingdom would have looked like and what it would have offered to theme park guests. An early piece of marketing material released by Disney gave details about Beastly Kingdom:

> Beastly Kingdom is the realm of make-believe animals, animals that don't really exist, out of legends, out of fairy tales, out of storybooks. Like our legends and fairy tales about imaginary animals, this land is divided into realms of good and realms of evil.
>
> The evil side is dominated by DRAGON'S TOWER, a burned, wrecked castle inhabited by a greedy, fire-breathing dragon. He hoards a fabulous treasure in his tower chamber. The castle is also inhabited by bats who speak to us from their upside down perches. The bats have a plan. They enlist our help trying to rob the dragon and fly us off on a wild chase. At last, we meet the fire-breathing dragon himself and barely escape un-barbecued.

> The good side of this land is ruled by QUEST OF THE UNICORN. An adventure which sends us through a maze of medieval mythological creatures to seek the hidden grotto where the unicorn lives. There is also FANTASIA GARDENS. A gentle musical boat ride through the animals from Disney's animated classic, *Fantasia*. Both the crocodiles and hippos from "Dance of the Hours" and the Pegasus, fauns and centaurs from Beethoven's "Pastoral" are found here.

Beastly Kingdom would have been visually stunning and divided into two separate and thematically distinct sub-areas. Upon entering Beastly Kingdom, guests would be faced with two different paths. First, a dark, winding path through a dense forest would lead to the "evil realm," at the center of which would be an ominous, crumbling stone castle. A second path would be lined with colorful and lush foliage leading to the "good realm" of Beastly Kingdom.

## The Evil Realm

A dark medieval village featuring buildings of rudimentary stone construction with thatched roofs, as well as an eerie courtyard with a Stone Henge-type geological arrangement, awaited those guests brave enough to travel down the ominous forest path to the evil realm of Beastly Kingdom. Towering high above the medieval village would have been a dramatic stone castle known as Dragon Tower.

Dragon Tower was not only supposed to be the signature attraction of Beastly Kingdom, but also the entire Animal Kingdom as a whole. It would have provided a much-needed thrill attraction for the park, and was supposed to be the primary reason that guests would initially rush there. It was supposed to be the park's "wienie."

Dragon Tower was to be an intricately themed and technologically advanced inverted roller coaster. This meant that the ride vehicles for the attraction would hang below the actual track, a first for Disney World.

Guests would begin their journey by travelling through the medieval village toward the ominous ruins of Dragon Tower. Scorched shields and armor, broken lances, and abandoned swords would line the walkways and the interior of the castle, a frightening reminder of the many failed attempts of knights and adventurers to defeat a sinister dragon. The show building itself would have been richly themed as a decrepit and crumbling stone castle long overtaken by a terrifying fire-breathing dragon, with its scorched façade and interior showing signs of the dragon's power.

As guests entered the decaying stronghold, they would travel through a dark interior filled with dust, cobwebs, and other clear indications that the castle had been long since abandoned by humans. Eventually, guests would encounter a series of audio-animatronic bats hanging upside down on a variety of interior perches. The bats would attempt to broker a deal with guests to steal the vast treasure trove of gold, jewels, and other riches hidden within the bowels of the tower. The only problem with the bats' proposal, as you probably guessed, was that a deadly fire-breathing dragon guarded the treasure. The bats would provide the much-needed comic relief to balance an otherwise dark and frightening experience.

After boarding the ride vehicles suspended below the coaster track, guests would travel through several "dark ride" scenes in the foreboding stronghold, including a variety of rooms in the castle as well as underground caverns. Guests would eventually reach a large treasure room and finally encounter the enormous fire-breathing dragon standing guard.

The dragon would have been the largest audio-animatronic ever constructed by Disney Imagineers and would have been nothing short of breathtaking. Not surprisingly, the dragon would awake just in time to discover that guests were conspiring to steal the treasure, and would send a real flame toward the ride vehicles before guests narrowly escaped the smoke-filled encounter. Dragon Tower would certainly have been an exhilarating experience for park guests.

## The Good Realm

Beastly Kingdom would have also included a "good realm" focused on mythical creatures of a more peaceful nature. This land would have featured opulent gardens filled with a variety of colorful flowers and numerous ponds, streams, and other water features. Buildings in this realm would be based on classic Greek architecture with wide columns and ornate carvings to create a captivating environment based on myth. Disney developed plans for two attractions in the good realm of Beastly Kingdom: Quest of the Unicorn and Fantasia Gardens.

One of the Animal Kingdom's more captivating experiences from a visual perspective would have been Quest for the Unicorn, a gorgeous hedge maze. Quest for the Unicorn would have been a walk-through guest experience featuring numerous interactive elements that guests would need to "unlock" in order to gain entry to the heart of the labyrinth. Along the way, guests would encounter numerous mythical animals, including centaurs and Pan-like creatures from mythology. As the name indicates, the maze would lead to a beautiful white unicorn in a quiet, picturesque underground grotto. Concept art for Quest for the Unicorn depicts lush landscaping and a variety of hidden paths and walkways.

Fantasia Gardens was to be a classic Disney "dark ride" that would have taken guests past scenes from the classic 1940 Disney animated feature film *Fantasia*. Set within an ornately themed show building with a Greek temple façade, guests would have travelled in boats similar to those used in It's a Small World and Pirates of the Caribbean. These boats would take guests past beautiful scenes of dancing hippos, ostriches, crocodiles, centaurs, and fauns as depicted in the "Dance of the Hours" and "Pastoral" segments of *Fantasia*. Fantasia Gardens would have been visually beautiful and relaxing, enjoyable by guests of all ages and standing in stark contrast to the Dragon Tower attraction.

## A Mythical Land Comes at a High Price

Despite the overwhelmingly positive feedback received from guests about a proposed Beastly Kingdom, it was not included when Animal Kingdom first opened on April 22, 1998. Disney Imagineers and executives felt that Animal Kingdom should first and foremost focus on "real" animals. With that emphasis as a starting point, the bulk of Disney's budget for Animal Kingdom was used to develop the Africa and Asia sections of the park, including two separate animal walking trails, the Pangani Forest Exploration Trail (now Gorilla Falls Exploration Trail) in Africa and the Maharajah Jungle Trek in Asia. The largest financial expenditure was the multi-million dollar Kilimanjaro Safaris. Covering more than one hundred acres, making it the largest Disney attraction in any park, Kilimanjaro Safaris offers guests an amazing tour past a wide variety of animals on an authentic African savanna.

The process of changing the central Florida landscape into an area suitable for animals from a wide variety of different environments was a challenging, expensive endeavor. It is estimated that Disney spent approximately $800 million in infrastructure, groundwork, and landscape for the entire park as well as development of the Africa and Asia sections of Animal Kingdom, specifically.

In his Letter to Shareholders that accompanied the 1998 Annual Report of The Walt Disney Company, then chairman and CEO Michael Eisner described the company's balancing act of trying to create wonderful guest experiences while also trying to grow profitability:

> All of our 1998 initiatives are geared toward [the goal of creating excellent guest entertainment]. Given their high quality and given the evidence that people all over the world will be enjoying more and more disposable time...in the years ahead, these investments have the potential to create significant growth down the road. Unfortunately, like all investments that create theoretical opportunities in the future, they cost *real* money right now.

Because of the substantial financial investment made on Africa and Asia, the already hemorrhaging Animal Kingdom budget only had room for one more category of animals. So what would it be, extinct dinosaurs or mythical dragons and unicorns? Ultimately, that decision was made based on a marketing push for the Disney computer-animated feature film *Dinosaur* (2000).

Disney poured a brontosaurs-sized amount of money into this film, and Disney executives were adamant about promoting *Dinosaur* in the company's newest theme park. With that, Disney moved forward with a land dedicated to dinosaurs, DinoLand, U.S.A., and a motion-based simulator attraction known as Countdown to Extinction (later renamed to DINOSAUR). As a result, there was no money left in the Animal Kingdom budget to construct Beastly Kingdom, and so it was moved to the "Phase Two" plans for the park, with a construction date no later than 2003.

Notwithstanding the delay, it appeared to be a foregone conclusion that Beastly Kingdom would eventually be incorporated into the park. After all, a theme park land dedicated to mythical beasts seems like an idea almost guaranteed to draw guests by the thousands. That sentiment was reflected in *Since the World Began, Walt Disney World The First 25 Years* (1996), where the plans for Animal Kingdom were featured as a standalone chapter. In reference to Beastly Kingdom, *Since the World Began* states:

> In this mythical world of unicorns, dragons, and other magical creatures, guests will come face to face with make-believe animals from legends, fairy tales, and storybooks—all of which play an important role in the circle of life because of their powerful hold on our imagination. The creatures will come to life through Disney's creative storytelling.

## A "Campy" Stand-In and Hope for the Future

With no hope of Beastly Kingdom being constructed for the opening day of Animal Kingdom, and plans for the Asia section of the park running behind schedule, the Disney company faced a big problem: the new park did not have enough attractions to accommodate expected crowd levels. To address this issue, Disney needed a land that was cheap, easy to implement, and easy to remove when the need arose. As a result, Camp Minnie-Mickey was quickly developed to help disperse crowds throughout the park.

Camp Minnie-Mickey featured a variety of character greeting locations and a stage show, but no actual attractions. Along with dealing with crowd concerns, Camp Minnie-Mickey would serve as a placeholder that could easily be removed when plans for Beastly Kingdom did move forward.

Despite this "campy" stand-in, all indications were that Beastly Kingdom would eventually be developed. The "mythical" component to Animal Kingdom was referenced in the 1996, 1997, and 1998 Annual Reports of

The Walt Disney Company, as well as in Michael Eisner's dedication of the park's opening (memorialized on its dedication plaque).

Once Animal Kingdom opened on April 22, 1998, Imagineers believed that the park would be a huge success and would generate substantial revenues. Its popularity would bring visitors to central Florida in droves, which would in turn increase attendance at the Magic Kingdom, Epcot, and Disney-MGM Studios. Based on this widespread success, Beastly Kingdom would be a certainty. But contrary to Disney's expectations, the presence of Animal Kingdom actually decreased attendance at Disney World's three other theme parks (a concept know as "cannibalizing").

Michael Eisner responded by moving forward with numerous attractions, shows, and parades at the Magic Kingdom, Epcot, and Disney-MGM Studios to increase attendance levels at those parks. But money was needed to pay for these additions. Where did Eisner find this money? Unfortunately, he found it in the coffers reserved for Animal Kingdom's Phase Two project, Beastly Kingdom. With this money now "re-dedicated" to other areas of Disney World, plans for Beastly Kingdom were once again delayed.

## Cheering for the Enemy

As strange as it may sound today, the Imagineers' hopes of getting Beastly Kingdom off the drawing board and into Animal Kingdom rested, for a time, with Disney's biggest competitor in the Orlando market, Universal Studios. In the late 1990s, Universal was pouring billions of dollars into widening its footprint in central Florida, including the creation of a new theme park called Islands of Adventure to pair with its already existing Universal Studios Florida park. Universal's goal was to incorporate multiple cutting-edge attractions that were so technologically advanced that they would blow away anything Disney World had to offer.

Imagineers hoped that Islands of Adventure would be the runaway hit that Universal Studios expected that it would be. Sound crazy? The rationale for this thinking was based on the ego of Michael Eisner and other Disney executives. If Islands of Adventure and its wide array of amazing attractions drew theme park guests away from the Disney parks, Disney executives would have no choice but to respond in kind by pouring money into new properties and attractions for its own parks.

Disney executives were so convinced that Islands of Adventure would be a success that Imagineers were ordered to develop a "contingency plan" that would be implemented if Disney World attendance fell as a result of Islands of Adventure. Along with other major additions to the Magic Kingdom, Epcot, and Disney-MGM Studios, the contingency plan included the long-awaited addition of Beastly Kingdom.

Islands of Adventure opened on May 28, 1999. As promised, the park included a wide variety of attractions that were technologically advanced and intricately themed, with many experiences geared more toward the adult thrill-seeker market. Islands of Adventure featured attractions such as The Amazing Adventures of Spider-Man, a revolutionary motion-based simulator attraction that remains near the top of many "best attractions" lists around the world; an Incredible Hulk roller coaster that featured a rapid launch mechanism that would send chills down the spine of even the most seasoned theme park fan; and The Jurassic Park River Adventure, a classic log flume-style ride themed to the lucrative *Jurassic Park* movie franchise.

The problem, for both Islands of Adventure and for Imagineers hoping for the opportunity to construct Beastly Kingdom, was that the crowds for Islands of Adventure never materialized as expected and the park's opening had almost no effect on Disney World attendance numbers. The reason for this flop is still unknown. Some believe that the theme park market was not ready for another stand-alone venue in central Florida. Others felt that the Universal Studios marketing team did a terrible job of clarifying for guests that Islands of Adventure would be a stand-alone park as opposed to just a separate land of the already existing Universal Studios Florida park.

Regardless of the reason for Islands' failure to bring in crowds as expected, the comprehensive "contingency plan" and the corresponding Disney capital expenditure was no longer needed. Because of this, Beastly Kingdom was once again placed on the proverbial shelf. Although the poor attendance numbers for Islands of Adventure again delayed Beastly Kingdom's construction, one of the themed "Islands" in Universal's newest park may have signaled its ultimate death knell.

## This Looks Very Familiar

The Lost Continent was one of the opening day themed lands in Islands of Adventure and featured a "myths and legends" motif. It consisted of buildings dramatically themed as stone ruins and Greek temples and featured experiences dedicated to mythical characters such as Poseidon and Sinbad.

The Lost Continent's starring attraction, Dueling Dragons, was a thrilling dual-tracked inverted roller coaster themed around dragons. Even worse, the queue for Dueling Dragons wound through a crumbling medieval castle. To add insult to injury, the Lost Continent also eventually included a child-focused roller coaster attraction known as the Flying Unicorn. Both of these attractions can still be enjoyed at Islands of Adventure today, but in very different thematic forms. When Harry Potter invaded Islands of Adventure in 2010, Dueling Dragons was re-themed as Dragon Challenge, and the Flying Unicorn was re-themed as Flight of the Hippogriff.

Rumor has it that Michael Eisner and other Disney executives took a covert trip to Islands of Adventure to look at their newest competition. During this visit, Eisner angrily observed that many concepts in the Lost Continent looked similar to what Disney had planned for Beastly Kingdom, especially the Dueling Dragons roller coaster. How did this happen? As is the case with many industries, employees of companies leave their current employers and get jobs for competitors on a regular basis. Imagineers are no exception. Following a rash of Disney layoffs, Universal hired many former Disney Imagineers, some of whom had worked on the conceptual plans for Beastly Kingdom. Knowing this, it is not surprising that dragon- and unicorn-based attractions originally planned for Disney's Animal Kingdom ended up in Islands of Adventure instead.

Unfortunately for Beastly Kingdom and the Imagineers who had worked tirelessly to develop its plans, there was no way that Disney executives, especially Eisner, were going to move forward with a land based on myth and legend when Universal had already done exactly that. As such, the already strained hopes for Beastly Kingdom quickly faded away.

## Finding Mythical Beasts in Disney's Animal Kingdom Today

While Beastly Kingdom never made it off the Imagineering drawing board and into Animal Kingdom, the park continues to embrace "imagined" animals. The *Imagineering Field Guide to Disney's Animal Kingdom at Walt Disney World* (2007) describes the influence mythical animals have on the park:

> The last story category [to be included in Disney's Animal Kingdom] is that of mythical animals and the various forms that they take. In truth, this group says more about humans than it does about animals—for it has to do with the attributes that we project onto animals. We assign them personality characteristics for us in our stories, such as referring to a lion, Simba, as the king of the animals, or holding a belief that a Yeti assumes the responsibility of protecting a mountain. This concept will continue to be developed over time.

Remnants of Beastly Kingdom can still be found in several areas of the park, most prominently in the Animal Kingdom logo which features silhouettes of five animals, including a lion, an elephant, and a triceratops. In the dead center of the logo, flanked by these real and extinct animals, is a dragon. This lineup of real, extinct, and imagined animals is also carved into a variety of benches throughout the park.

Another vestige of Beastly Kingdom can be seen as soon as guests pull their vehicles into the Animal Kingdom parking areas. One of the many parking lots is named "Unicorn" and features a sign with a prancing unicorn. Once guests have parked, they encounter a second and more dramatic Beastly Kingdom tribute when purchasing tickets, as a menacing dragon's head stands guard over one of Animal Kingdom's ticket booths.

For years, guests could also observe "forbidding Dragon Rocks" (a dragon-shaped rock formation) on the banks of the Discovery River. The stone dragon could be seen on the bridge entering Camp Minnie-Mickey and at times actually spewed water into the river. It was a nice find for curious theme park guests, especially those longing for Beastly Kingdom to become a reality. Due to a massive expansion of Disney's Animal Kingdom discussed below, it is unclear at this point whether this stone dragon will survive.

Another tribute could be seen when the Discovery River Boat Tour (which was referred to by many different names through the years) still plied Animal Kingdom's Discovery River. On this journey, guests could see a cave on the banks of the river from which erupted a dragon's roar and an occasional burst of flame. Imagineers originally planned for an actual dragon's head to peek out of the cave, as well as several other previews for Beastly Kingdom. Unfortunately, budget constraints prevented these additions from happening. The Discovery River Boat Tour closed in 1999.

Luckily for fans of thrill rides and mythical beasts, Imagineers developed Expedition Everest in 2006 for the Asia section of the park. Expedition Everest is a roller coaster set within a massive mountainous landscape, and features an encounter with the mythical guardian of the mountain, the Yeti. It is the park's "wienie," drawing thousands of guests each day.

A Fantasia Gardens does exist in Walt Disney World. However, it is not an indoor boat attraction sailing past scenes from *Fantasia*. Instead, Fantasia Gardens is a miniature golf course that first opened in 1996 and features a variety of dancing hippos and alligators, as well as other scenes from the classic 1940 Disney film.

After more than a decade, Disney finally made the decision to close Camp Minnie-Mickey to make room for the addition of a new land of fantastic mythical creatures and jaw-dropping landscapes. In 2011, Disney made the blockbuster announcement that it had reached an agreement with director James Cameron to, among other things, develop a new land for Animal Kingdom themed to Cameron's massively successful 2009 film *Avatar*. Construction is now well underway on Pandora: The World of Avatar in the area where Camp Minnie-Mickey once stood. The project is the largest expansion ever for Animal Kingdom, and will include the famous floating mountains from the film, as well as representations of Pandora's natives, the Nav'i. Pandora: The World of Avatar is expected to open in 2017.

CHAPTER SIXTEEN

# Animal Kingdom Icons

*The stakes are very high any time we work on an attraction that is to go into one of our park icons. Such an attraction carries with it the weight of defining the park's concept, or at least to justify its placement in such a high-profile location!*

— The Imagineers, *The Imagineering Field Guide to Disney's Animal Kingdom at Walt Disney World* (2007)

Each of Walt Disney World's four major theme parks has an "icon," a stunning visual landmark that symbolizes the story, theme, and atmosphere of the Magic Kingdom, Epcot, Hollywood Studios, and Animation Kingdom. Perhaps the most recognizable theme park icon in the entire world is Cinderella Castle in the Magic Kingdom, a gorgeous 189-foot tall castle straight out of the pages of a classic fairy tale. Cinderella Castle embodies the joy, hope, innocence, and adventure represented throughout the Magic Kingdom.

Epcot's icon is Spaceship Earth, a captivating 180-foot tall geodesic sphere (not a large golf ball). Spaceship Earth houses an attraction about the history and development of human communication, and symbolizes the wonder, imagination, discovery, and spirit of human achievement.

The icon for Hollywood Studios is admittedly more complicated. For years, the enormous Sorcerer's Hat from the 1940 animated film *Fantasia* served as the park's icon, to the horror of many Disney fans. The Sorcerer's Hat was removed from the park in January of 2015. The park's current icon is The Great Movie Ride, housed in a dramatic re-creation of Grauman's Chinese Theatre (now known as TCL Chinese Theatre) that sits at the end of Hollywood Boulevard and represents the Golden Era of Hollywood.

The Tree of Life serves as the icon for Animal Kingdom. Standing at 145 feet tall, it dramatically embodies the concepts of nature, wildlife, conservation, and the diversity of animal species. As is the case with other park icons, the Tree of Life is synonymous with Animal Kingdom, and it is difficult to imagine the park without it. However, during the planning process for the park, Imagineers considered a number of different options for its icon, including a one-of-a-kind carousel that would have allowed guests to travel on land, sail on water, and soar through the sky, and a mammoth re-creation of Noah's Ark.

## Animal Kingdom Carousel

Early plans for Disney's Animal Kingdom called for the park's icon to be a carousel. While that may sound disappointing initially, this was not going to be a "normal" carousel. Instead, the Animal Kingdom carousel was to be a one-of-a kind attraction that would have been both visually stunning and entertaining. It would have consisted of three separate levels representing three broad animal groups and offering three completely different ride experiences.

The base level of the carousel would represent animal species that lived or spent significant time in water. Guests would have been able to sail around a large circular pool in boats intricately themed to a wide variety of animals including a sea otter, tortoise, and hippopotamus. In the middle of the pool, a large whale would support an equally large lotus blossom leaf, which would in turn serve as the foundation for the second level of the carousel.

The second level would represent animal species living on the land. This portion of the attraction would have appeared very similar to normal carousels, with children and children-at-heart travelling on animals in a circular motion. Instead of horses, however, the ride vehicles would have been in the form of such mammals as elephants, giraffes, lions, and rhinos.

The third and final level of the Animal Kingdom carousel would have been devoted to birds of flight. Guests would have travelled in ride vehicles in a classic hub-and-spoke style similar to the Astro Orbiter in Tomorrowland, Dumbo the Flying Elephant in Fantasyland, and the Magic Carpets of Aladdin in Adventureland. The ride vehicles for the top level of the carousel would have included a peacock, a butterfly, a swan, and a number of other exotic birds.

Eventually, Imagineers scrapped plans for the three-tiered carousel due to word coming down from the man then in charge of the Disney company, Michael Eisner. In *The Making of Disney's Animal Kingdom Theme Park* (1998), Melody Malmberg quotes Imagineer Joe Rohde in describing Eisner's decision: "[Eisner] thought it was too frivolous."

Another contributing factor to the carousel being shelved was its size. While a three-tiered carousel would certainly have been large when compared to other carousel-type attractions, it probably would not have been large enough to justify serving as the Animal Kingdom's icon when compared to the icons of other parks such as Cinderella Castle and Spaceship Earth.

## Noah's Ark

One of the most intriguing initial concepts proposed for Animal Kingdom was a replica of Noah's Ark that would have served as the entrance to the park. It would have not only been an awe-inspiring icon, but also one of the most visually stunning structures ever constructed in any Disney theme park.

An early artistic rendering of this concept by Imagineer Joe Rohde depicts an enormous ark, appearing as though it had been shipwrecked, with a wide pathway running through a large hole in the ship's hull. This path would have served as the primary entrance point for Animal Kingdom.

The grand size of the Noah's Ark concept cannot be understated. As it would have served as the primary entrance, with thousands of guests passing through each day, the ark would have had to be enormous.

Once inside the park, guests would enter an area known as Genesis Gardens, a lushly landscaped and heavily vegetated area used to showcase a number of exotic plants and unique landscaping elements intended to evoke thoughts of an undisturbed Garden of Eden.

Similar to the Oasis, the area of Disney's Animal Kingdom that guests first encounter when entering the park today, the ark would have featured a number of animal encounter displays setting the stage for the rest of the park (although it is unlikely that the ark would have displayed two animals of every species).

The proposed concepts of Noah's Ark and Genesis Gardens would have fit well conceptually with the story of Animal Kingdom by representing the themes of conservation, the wide variety of animal species, and lush and exotic landscaping. It would have also accomplished the goal of creating a visually stunning landmark and resonating symbol for the park. So why did the ark concept never make it off the drawing board? While no definitive reason has been given, the religious connotations associated with the project most likely played a role in it being docked.

## The Tree of Life

Imagineers eventually decided to construct a Tree of Life as the Animal Kingdom's park icon. However, early iterations were far different than what eventually opened with the park on April 22, 1998. One early conceptual design for the Tree of Life would have allowed guests to actually ascend to an observation deck that would have been located at the top of the tree. Imagine standing at the peak of the Tree of Life at dusk and observing Discovery Island and the rest of the park as a whole from that amazing vantage point!

Although the family-friendly 3D theatre experience It's Tough to Be a Bug currently entertains guests at the base of the Tree of Life, early plans called for a restaurant to be housed within the roots of the tree. Appropriately named "Roots," this restaurant would have been "the Park's finest eatery." The concept was abandoned when Imagineers made the decision to incorporate an attraction there instead.

Imagineers considered multiple options for the attraction in an effort to accurately capture the spirit of Animal Kingdom. The *Imagineering Field Guide to Disney's Animal Kingdom at Walt Disney World* (2007) describes this process:

> The subject matter varied in style and tone, from majestic tributes to the wonders of nature, to character-driven fables....

Disney Imagineers developed concept art for two separate attractions. One was based on the 1994 Disney animated film *The Lion King*. Another idea was for a "wonders of nature" attraction where an actual "Mother Nature" would lead guests on a series of adventures. However, the Imagineers did not feel that either of these concepts accurately captured the spirit of Animal Kingdom. Eventually, they developed a 3D film attraction based on the 1998 Pixar film *A Bug's Life* that opened with the park in that same year.

## Remnants of Early Concepts

Thousands of guests stare in awe and amazement each day when they enter Animal Kingdom and see the Tree of Life at the center of Discovery Island. *The Imagineering Field Guide to Disney's Animal Kingdom at Walt Disney World* (2007) describes this amazing achievement:

> The Tree of Life is one of the most amazing pieces of art ever created by WDI [Walt Disney Imagineering]. It's beautiful and meaningful, and captures the essence of this park at a glance. It's a poetic statement of the majesty of nature, the stunning diversity of animals, and our respect for our place in the world, and underscores the ideal that all of these elements can co-exist harmoniously. In our story, the animals are not carved into the surface—they've grown out from it. As one approaches the tree and the animal forms begin to reveal themselves, it becomes clear that there is almost no tree at all. That tree *is* the animal kingdom.

While guests can't dine in a fine restaurant at the base of the Tree of Life, and they have to travel to the Africa section of the park to see a show about *The Lion King*. In addition, the 3D theatre show that currently sits at the base of the Tree of Life, It's Tough to Be a Bug, combines 3D effects, an impressive audio-animatronic villain, and several other surprises to create a hilarious family-friendly experience.

Guests in Disney World today can find a carousel in the Fantasyland section of the Magic Kingdom in the form of the Prince Charming Regal Carrousel (formerly known as Cinderella's Golden Carrousel). Unlike the proposed Animal Kingdom Carousel, however, the Fantasyland version is a traditional carousel first created by the Philadelphia Toboggan Company in 1917 and featuring a variety of horses for young princes and princesses to enjoy.

For guests wanting to ride a carousel featuring non-traditional ride vehicles (horses), King Triton's Carousel of The Sea in Disney California Adventure simulates an adventure, appropriately enough, under the sea. Themed to the 1989 Disney animated film *The Little Mermaid*, the carousel allows guests to ride aboard dolphins, whales, sea horses, sea lions, and other ocean creatures.

The closest ride experience to the three-tiered carousel planned for Animal Kingdom, however, is found far from central Florida in Tokyo DisneySea, Disney's highly themed park in Japan. The Caravan Carousel featured in that park has a strong Arabian theme and, most distinctly, a two-story construction that allows guests to ride on a combination of horses and characters from the 1992 Disney animated film *Aladdin* on two separate levels.

CHAPTER SEVENTEEN

# The Excavator

*The most imposing presence in town is that of the Dino Institute, which houses the DINOSAUR attraction. The institute was founded when the mother lode of dinosaur fossils reared its flattened and petrified head.*

— The Imagineers, *The Imagineering Field Guide to Disney's Animal Kingdom at Walt Disney World Resort* (2007)

Expedition Everest—Legend of the Forbidden Mountain is a 199-foot tall roller coaster that races around and through a mysterious Himalayan mountain and dominates the skyline of Disney's Animal Kingdom. This headliner attraction opened on April 7, 2006, approximately eight years after the Animal Kingdom opened to guests on April 22, 1998. Everest features a unique combination of extremely detailed theming, an elaborate backstory, and an exhilarating ride experience on a speeding roller coaster.

Although it remains one of the most popular attractions in all of Walt Disney World, it was not the first roller coaster proposed for Animal Kingdom. That honor goes to the Excavator, an old-fashioned wooden roller coaster that was originally planned for the DinoLand, U.S.A section of Animal Kingdom. Much like the dinosaurs represented throughout DinoLand, however, plans for the Excavator are now extinct. But instead of a giant asteroid impact, a catastrophic seismic shift, or a massive volcanic eruption, the Excavator's extinction rested with enormous budgetary overruns faced by the Disney company during construction of the Animal Kingdom and a corporate push to include more child-friendly attractions.

## DinoLand, U.S.A.

From the beginning, Disney Imagineers knew that the Animal Kingdom would be "a kingdom of animals...real, ancient and imagined; a kingdom ruled by lions, dinosaurs and dragons." Dinosaurs are, not surprisingly, represented in the DinoLand, U.S.A. section of the Animal Kingdom. *The*

*Making of Disney's Animal Kingdom Theme Park* (1998) by Melody Malmberg described DinoLand, U.S.A as "a tribute to our American love of dinosaurs, from tacky roadside attractions to serious scientific inquiry."

The story of the Excavator begins with the backstory of DinoLand, U.S.A. as a whole. This backstory dates back to the 1940s in a small town off of Highway 498 in fictional Diggs County, primarily known as a place of quiet relaxation and good fishing. The town was also home to a small gas station run by an elderly couple, Chester and Hester, who sold basic necessities such as gas, snacks, and fishing supplies.

Notwithstanding its calm beginnings, the town's history was forever changed when a massive cache of dinosaur fossils was unexpectedly discovered. Professors specializing in areas such as anthropology, archaeology, and paleontology soon flooded the town, and their young and mischievous graduate students followed. Eventually, the prestigious Dino Institute was established:

> The denizens of this bastion of higher learning are deeply devoted to the science of dinosaurs, and don't have much of a sense of humor about their work. They're stuffy and self-important, and... institutional.

With the influx of both people and notoriety to the area, Chester and Hester looked to capitalize on the opportunity to make more money and began selling dinosaur souvenirs out of their gas station. The couple even went so far as to create an amusement park known as Chester and Hester's Dino-Rama. This area stands in stark contrast to the formal and stuffy atmosphere of the Dino Institute, and is reminiscent of a bright, tacky roadside carnival featuring midway-style games, flashing neon lights, and an array of loud colors and billboards.

## Plans for the Excavator

The key event in DinoLand, U.S.A's history is obviously the discovery of dinosaur fossils. This is where the Excavator would have come into play. DinoLand's backstory would have been slightly modified to incorporate a mining and/or sand-and-gravel company operating in the town. The operation included a massive mechanical piece of machinery known as the Excavator, which would send ore carts in and out of the mine/gravel pits.

During an otherwise normal day of "digging" operations by this company, one of the largest archaeological finds in the history of the world was discovered in the form of an enormous deposit of dinosaur bones. Due to this monumental discovery, the company's commercial operations were abandoned, including the Excavator. Years later, those mischievous graduate students who followed their professors to DinoLand, U.S.A decided to turn the Excavator back on, despite the machine having broken down and now being in a state of almost complete disrepair.

If the Excavator would have been constructed in Animal Kingdom, guests would have encountered numerous warning signs when approaching the attraction such as "DANGER" and "DO NOT ENTER." This would have emphasized the theming of an abandoned mining operation where the equipment had long since failed and any person approaching the site was putting their life at risk.

Although plans for the Excavator were never fully developed, three pieces of conceptual artwork help us understand what the ride experience would have been like. The first illustration is a conceptual rendering of a portion of DinoLand, U.S.A. by artist James Wong that is focused on the Boneyard, an elaborate sandbox area for children themed as a large dinosaur fossil dig area. The foreground of the illustration shows children playing and exploring around a sandlot playground with different dinosaur skeletons scattered about the area. In the background of the picture, almost as an afterthought, is a large wooden roller coaster, complete with ride vehicles cresting a large lift hill. A mound of dirt, perhaps even a mountain, is shown directly beside the Excavator's lift hill. It is unclear from the perspective of this drawing whether the coaster track actually goes through the dirt hill or runs behind it.

The second conceptual depiction of the Excavator is more menacing, and is a close-up of the coaster ride vehicles, old mining carts, racing through a specific section of the Excavator's track. The track itself is composed of old wooden timbers decaying from years of neglect, with grass and moss now encroaching on the machine's operation. Even more concerning is that the coaster runs directly through a dinosaur skeleton, with hazy beams of sunshine eerily passing through the reptile's skull. In one section, the dinosaur's enormous ribs actually enclose the coaster's track in grim semi-circles.

The third illustration of the proposed Excavator coaster also includes a dinosaur, but one of a much different nature. Rather than an actual dinosaur skeleton, this beast is a piece of folksy artwork, specifically, old metal scraps, gears, and even the body of a junkyard truck that have been artfully combined to create a dinosaur statue reminiscent of a corny roadside tourist attraction. In this illustration, the Excavator's ride vehicles race by the statue, with passengers shown in a frightened state either due to the speed of the coaster or the sight of this "junkosaurus rex." This type of structure would have been right at home in the Chester and Hester section of the park.

## "Extinction Level" Events

An adrenaline-pumping roller coaster themed as a "dig site" would seem to be a welcome addition to Animal Kingdom and a perfect fit for DinoLand, U.S.A. So why did it never come to be? First, the tremendous budgetary overruns that the Disney company faced during the construction of Animal Kingdom were significant. Disney poured millions of dollars into developing the Africa and Asia sections of the park, finding out the hard way that creating, organizing, and maintaining theme park areas where real animals would live and breathe was both more difficult and more expensive than anyone originally contemplated. These budgetary constraints were the primary reason that Disney initially delayed its plans for the hotly anticipated Beastly Kingdom section of the park. Unfortunately, the cost overruns were so significant that cutting Beastly Kingdom from the opening day plans was not enough, and the Excavator soon also found itself on the "extinct" attraction concepts list.

Another factor that contributed to the Excavator not being added to Animal Kingdom after the park opened on April 22, 1998, was a growing concern within the Disney company that its newest park did not have enough attractions for children. On the Animal Kingdom's opening day, the park included twelve attractions, including Kilimanjaro Safaris, Countdown to Extinction, Festival of the Lion King, It's Tough to be a Bug, and Rafiki's Planet Watch. Many of these experiences were focused on either adult entertainment or wildlife education and enrichment, which did not particularly appeal to Disney's younger park guests. As DinoLand, U.S.A. already featured Countdown to Extinction (later renamed to DINOSAUR), a thrilling attraction that takes guests on an adventure back in time to rescue a dinosaur, Imagineers did not think that another adult-focused attraction was needed to draw guests to that section of the park. These factors were "extinction level" events which caused plans for the Excavator to be buried permanently.

## Excavator "Fossils" in the Parks Today

Although DinoLand, U.S.A. never got the Excavator, it did get a roller coaster in 2002 called Primeval Whirl, located in the Chester and Hester's Dino-Rama section of DinoLand, and, not surprisingly, festooned with bright lights and tacky signage. Primeval Whirl is loosely themed as a time machine, but that theming is easily lost given the surrounding atmosphere. However, what sets Primeval Whirl apart from other roller coasters is that the ride vehicles themselves actually spin throughout the attraction.

Animal Kingdom is also home to the Boneyard, which Disney describes as "[a]n open air play space designed to look like a dinosaur dig site where kids can explore and have fun." The Excavator has a couple of connections to the Boneyard. First, both attractions center on the discovery of dinosaur bones. Second, and more specifically, the Boneyard was clearly depicted in one of the above-discussed conceptual illustrations featuring the Excavator.

Roller-coaster enthusiasts who long for the days of the Excavator were given an even better gift on April 7, 2006, when Expedition Everest opened in Animal Kingdom. Everest is one of the most popular, most intricately themed, and most exciting attractions ever created by Disney Imagineers. Instead of racing past a grim dinosaur skeleton, guests riding Expedition Everest instead pass by a large, roaring Yeti, the guardian of Forbidden Mountain.

Finally, park guests who want to ride a roller coaster through the skeletal remains of a dinosaur can still, believe it or not, find just such an experience in the Magic Kingdom. Big Thunder Mountain Railroad is a runaway mine train roller coaster that races around, over, and through an intricately detailed Monument Valley landscape in the Frontierland section of the Magic Kingdom. On this journey, which is described as the "wildest ride in the wilderness," guests race past a series of unearthed dinosaur fossils.

PART FIVE

# Resorts

*Resort hotels will become increasingly important in the years ahead. We plan to open at least nine more hotels in Florida during the Disney Decade. Combined with our new convention facilities, they will add greatly to Walt Disney World's attractiveness as a meeting and convention site.*

— 1990 Annual Report, The Walt Disney Company

CHAPTER EIGHTEEN

# Lost Resorts

*Five "International" hotels that symbolize Walt Disney World's thematic concept are being planned for development in Phase One...the first five years of the Vacation Kingdom's growth.*

— "Preview Edition, Walt Disney World, 'The Vacation Kingdom of the World'" (1970)

Three iconic resorts sit on the picturesque shores of the Seven Seas Lagoon literally steps away from the Magic Kingdom: Disney's Contemporary Resort, Disney's Polynesian Village Resort, and Disney's Grand Floridian Resort & Spa. The Contemporary is an unmistakable architectural marvel. With its dramatic A-frame construction and ultra-modern feel (despite being over forty years old), complete with a monorail running through its center, the Contemporary appears as though it were pulled directly from the pages of a science-fiction novel. It opened with the Magic Kingdom on October 1, 1971, along with Disney's Polynesian Village Resort.

In contrast to the Contemporary, the Polynesian is themed as a tropical island paradise. Its lush landscaping, numerous water features, and relaxing atmosphere combine to create a stunning South Pacific-style resort complex.

The Grand Floridian opened almost two decades after the Contemporary and the Polynesian. With its white building façade, distinctive red roof, numerous fine-dining options, and a stunning multi-level lobby complete with a live symphony orchestra, the Grand Floridian exudes Victorian-era elegance and sophistication.

With their intricate and distinctive theming, luxurious guest offerings, and prime geographic locations, the Contemporary, Polynesian, and Grand Floridian are three of the most popular resorts in all of Walt Disney World. Unbeknownst to many, however, Disney's original plans called for five "themed" resorts that would sit on the shores of the Seven Seas Lagoon, not three. Even more surprisingly, the Grand Floridian was not included in those initial plans.

Three additional signature resort hotels themed in Thai, Italian, and Persian motifs were supposed to have joined the Contemporary and Polynesian as the flagship resorts for the Magic Kingdom. Unfortunately, an oil embargo half a world away forced the Disney company to drastically change its original plans.

## Phase One Plans

Disney's initial "Phase One" plans (scheduled for completion during the first five years) for Disney World included five themed resorts, so designated "because everything from interior décor to employees' costumes and dining room menus will carry out an overall theme."

Disney's plans were made clear by virtue of numerous preview publications and materials published prior to the opening of the Magic Kingdom. For example, in the "Preview Edition, Walt Disney World, 'The Vacation Kingdom of the World,'" an early Disney marketing booklet published in 1970, Disney stated that:

> Surrounding [the Magic Kingdom], strung out like separate jewels on a necklace, are the major "theme resorts" of Walt Disney World. Although each is distinct in the architectural and cultural concept it represents, the resort hotels are interlaced by a network of land and water transportation systems. In Walt Disney World, distant Asia and the island world of Polynesia are but minutes apart.

The Contemporary and the Polynesian would open with the Magic Kingdom in 1971. The Asian Resort, the Venetian Resort, and the Persian Resort would then follow:

> Additional resort hotels, themed from around the world, will be developed along the shores of the picturesque lake and lagoon according to future demand. Already being planned are the Thai-inspired Asian resort, the exotic Persian-style and the Venetian....

Disney executives envisioned that this collection of resorts would not only provide needed rooms for the thousands of theme park guests expected at Disney World, but would be experiences in and of themselves that would draw guests to the parks:

> Each hotel will be a complete major attraction in itself, with its own recreation activities, entertainment, dining facilities, and resort atmosphere. Additionally, guests in any hotel will be able to enjoy facilities of all others and the attractions of the entire "Vacation Kingdom" during their stay.

Disney was so sure that the Asian, Venetian, and Persian Resorts would be constructed that the front cover of the "Preview Edition" featured a brilliant artistic rendering of the Seven Seas Lagoon complete with depictions of each of these three resorts along with the Contemporary and the Polynesian on the lagoon's shores. This same depiction was also included as a full-page illustration in the 1969 Annual Report of Walt Disney Productions.

## Asian Resort

Of the three "themed" resorts that never were, the Asian was the closest to becoming a reality. It would have been located on the shores of the Seven Seas Lagoon in approximately the same location that the Grand Floridian sits today. Conceptual drawings and overhead pictures of the Seven Seas Lagoon during this time period show a large square piece of land extending into the lagoon that would have served as the foundation for the Asian Resort.

Thanks to detailed descriptions in various marketing materials produced by the Disney company, we know a great deal about the appearance, structure, and offerings of the proposed Asian Resort. "A Complete Edition About Walt Disney World, 'The Vacation Kingdom of the World,'" a marketing publication released by Disney in 1969, gave a broad overview of the entire Disney World project, including this description of the Asian Resort:

> The Asian-style hotel is primarily Thai in its décor and food specialties. Two-thirds of its 600 rooms are planned "on the water" or in garden settings—the remainder will be in a 160-foot high tower building, overlooking the lagoon and a central recreation area.

The "Preview Edition, Walt Disney World, 'The Vacation Kingdom of the World'" (1970) provided additional information:

> The Asian hotel will be strongly Thai in its motif. A theme restaurant and lounge at the top of its 160-foot tower building will provide an enchanting setting for nighttime dancing and stage show entertainment. Each of its 600 rooms, including 50 elegant suites in royal Thai décor, will look out on the lagoon or a central recreation area.

In conformity with the piece of land upon which the hotel complex would have been built, the Asian Resort would have been a large square in shape. As set forth in the above descriptions, and as depicted in numerous artistic renderings, a grand 160-foot tall tower composed of four large A-frame widows would sit at the center of the property and serve as the visual marquee for the resort. A grand restaurant would be housed inside this central tower offering a wide variety of Thai cuisine. The restaurant would have been breathtaking, with high ceilings and dramatic views from each of the A-frame windows. More than just a simple dining experience, the restaurant would have also provided "stage-show entertainment" each night for guests. One can only imagine how exciting this entertainment would have been given the dramatic setting of the restaurant itself and the strong Thai cultural influence. In addition to the restaurant, the central tower building of the Asian would have also included approximately two hundred guest rooms.

Long rows of guest buildings would have surrounded the central tower building along the outer border of the property, creating a beautiful central courtyard. These guest buildings would provide an additional four hundred guest rooms. The resort would have been surrounded by water on three sides, offering many rooms with grand views of the Seven Seas Lagoon and in some cases the Magic Kingdom.

The Asian would have offered a full range of guest services, including a highly themed swimming pool area as well as convention facilities. Interestingly enough, the "Complete Edition" preview guide noted that '[a] ll convention facilities will be underneath and separated from the main public areas."

A monorail station separate from the main resort buildings would provide guests with transportation from the resort to the Magic Kingdom, the Ticket and Transportation Center, and the other resort hotels located on the Magic Kingdom monorail loop.

The "Preview Edition" noted that the Contemporary and the Polynesian resorts would open in the first year of Walt Disney's World operation, while the Asian would "follow later in the Phase One plan." Disney was so sure that the Asian Resort would be constructed that it actually named a nearby service road Asian Way. This road was later renamed, for reasons that will be explained later, to Floridian Way.

## Venetian Resort

Disney also planned a grand Italian-themed hotel complex known as the Venetian. It would have been located on the shores of the Seven Seas Lagoon between the Contemporary and the Ticket and Transportation Center. "A Complete Edition About Walt Disney World 'The Vacation Kingdom of the World'" (1969) gave the following details about the Venetian:

> In the style of St. Mark's Square, the 500-room Venetian theme resort will be strongly oriented to water activities. It will feature an enclosed small boat harbor, entered from the lagoon area, and an intricate system of waterways designed to create the atmosphere of Venice."

"The Preview Edition Walt Disney World 'The Vacation Kingdom of the World'" (1970) elaborated:

> At the Venetian resort, an enclosed small boat harbor and intricate system of waterways will re-create the old world charm of the famed Italian "City of Canals." Shopping will be a very unique experience as guests travel by gondola along "streets of water" and under ornate bridges linking various sections of the resort. The style is reminiscent of St. Mark's Square, complete with a 120-foot campanile which will toll the time. The entire lobby will be glass-topped, creating a brilliant, sunlit atrium effect indoors.

One can only imagine the beauty and grace that would have been exuded in the Venetian Resort, with guests having the opportunity to travel by gondola through numerous interconnected waterways around the hotel grounds. The Venetian would also been in contention for the most romantic resort on Disney World property. After all, what could be more romantic at Disney World (or anywhere else) than riding a gondola around a beautiful resort en route to fine Italian dining and shopping?

The Venetian would have also featured its own monorail station providing guests with access to the Magic Kingdom, Ticket and Transportation Center, and surrounding resort hotels. As was the case with the Asian, the Venetian Resort was to open at some point during Disney World's "Phase One" plan.

## Persian Resort

The Persian, the third proposed "themed" resort that never came to be at Walt Disney World, may have very well been the most distinct. "A Complete Edition About Walt Disney World, 'The Vacation Kingdom of the World'" (1969) described the proposed resort:

> Located on the lake, the Persian-style hotel will create the effect of visiting an exotic far eastern palace. Crowning the central lobby will be a colossal dome, from which balconies will radiate to the 500 rooms. Accommodations will look out over the lake or onto beautifully landscaped courtyards.

"The Preview Edition, Walt Disney World, 'The Vacation Kingdom of the World'" (1970) added:

> Stepping right out of the *Arabian Nights* is the Persian resort which will reign like an exotic far-Eastern palace on the Northwest shore of the lake. Jewel-like mosques and columns will rise above landscaped courtyards, while terraced sundecks offer sculptured swimming pools and "old Persian" dining facilities. Guests will practically be able to sail to their own rooms through a sheltered marina.

The Persian Resort was to be located north of Disney's Contemporary and just outside the Magic Kingdom railroad adjacent to Tomorrowland.

As depicted in gorgeous conceptual renderings for the proposed development, the Persian would have featured a stunning twenty-four foot tall blue dome sitting atop an octagonal-shaped central lobby building. This stunning architectural feature would have certainly drawn stares from every corner of the Seven Seas Lagoon. The resort complex would have also featured seven smaller blue domes incorporated into the surrounding buildings that would form an octagonal shape around the central structure. The entire Persian Resort would be gorgeously splashed in bright white and blue colors, creating both an exciting and refreshing atmosphere.

As is the case with Disney's Polynesian Village, guest buildings and approximately five hundred guest rooms would have radiated out from the beautiful central structure of the Persian.

Like the Asian and Venetian resorts, the Persian would have also provided guests with access to the monorail. Different conceptual drawings show different ways in which this would have been accomplished, either through a spur from the main monorail track, or alternatively by virtue of a second monorail loop that would have actually gone through Tomorrowland in the Magic Kingdom! In fact, the monorail may have actually travelled through the Persian in much the same way as it does the Contemporary.

As was the case with the Asian and the Venetian, the Persian Resort was to open during the Phase One timeline for Walt Disney World.

In addition to the pre-opening marketing materials published by Disney, the proposed Asian, Venetian, and Persian resorts were also featured on an early "Fun Map" of the Magic Kingdom and the Seven Seas Lagoon by artist Paul Hartley and featured in both *The Story of Walt Disney World, Commemorative Edition, A Behind-the-Scenes Visit to the Vacation Kingdom* (1971) and *The Art of Walt Disney World Resort* (2009). On this map, Hartley "has purposefully distorted the locations of landmarks and their relationships to each other for the sake of a more pleasing design." The map provides an exaggerated layout of the Magic Kingdom and the surrounding resorts, including the "Future Asian Resort—Hotel," "Future Venetian Resort—Hotel," and "Future Persian Resort—Hotel."

## Grand Plans Put on Hold

The beautiful theming and immersive atmospheres of the Asian, Venetian, and Persian resorts would have almost certainly been a big success with theme park guests. Given both the quantity and specificity of the details provided by Disney in the "Preview Edition" and the "Complete Guide" about these resorts, as well as the numerous conceptual drawings included therein and elsewhere, it is clear that Disney planned on moving forward with these projects during the Phase One timeline for Walt Disney World.

In the case of the Asian Resort, Disney made clear in the 1972 Annual Report for Walt Disney Productions (the predecessor entity to the Disney company) that construction would begin in 1974:

> Since opening day, the demand for accommodations throughout central Florida has exceeded the supply. On site, our two theme resort-hotels, the Contemporary and the Polynesian Village, operated at near 100% capacity all year long. Our two hotels and the Fort Wilderness Campground together hosted 1,750,000 guests during the year.... Recognizing, however, that the public will always prefer to stay within the "Vacation Kingdom" site, the Company will soon begin architectural work on a third theme resort, the 500-room [the "Preview Edition" had stated 600 rooms; this may be a downgrading of the project] Asian Hotel. Construction is planned for 1974, with the formal opening to take place late that year.

Given the clear early intent of Disney to move forward with these projects, why were they never constructed? Unfortunately, the three resorts fell victim to the tumultuous economic environment that resulted from a 1973 oil embargo.

In October 1973, literally days removed from the two year anniversary of Walt Disney World, OPEC implemented what it called "oil diplomacy." Specifically, OPEC prohibited any nation that had supported Israel in the Yom Kippur War with Egypt, Syria, and Jordan from buying any of the oil it sold. This embargo included the United States. Thereafter, the price of oil skyrocketed, resulting in a worldwide energy crisis and a crash of the New York Stock Exchange. This, in turn, ushered in one of the worst recessions in United States history.

Disney had the difficult job explaining the significant negative impact of the energy crisis on attendance numbers for the parks in its 1974 Annual Report:

> Inflation, the crisis of confidence in government and the prolonged concern about the availability of gasoline had a profound effect upon business activity in the United States, and our Company felt the impact of these conditions, as did everyone else.

Families were simply too concerned with economic conditions in general and gas prices specifically to make their annual trips to Walt Disney World. For these reasons, attendance numbers for Disney World declined significantly and, as a result, many plans for future development, including additional resorts on property, were placed on hold. To the extent Disney did spend money on projects in the coming years, these dollars were devoted to attractions and parks (Epcot) that would push guests to visit Disney World and stay in the resorts that were already open for business.

## The Grand Floridian, the Mediterranean, and a Sinking Foundation

In 1988, seventeen years following the opening of the Contemporary and the Polynesian Village, Disney finally moved forward with adding a highly themed luxury resort on the shores of the Seven Seas Lagoon. However, instead of the Asian, Venetian, or Persian, a new resort known as the Grand Floridian Beach Resort (later renamed to Disney's Grand Floridian Resort & Spa) opened its doors to Disney guests.

The Grand Floridian was constructed on a reconfigured version of the large square piece of land originally planned for the Asian. Themed as an elegant seaside resort from the late nineteenth century, the Grand Floridian was an immediate success and continues to be one of the most popular and most expensive resorts on Disney World property.

Following the overwhelming success of the Grand Floridian, Michael Eisner, then the chairman and CEO of the Disney company, wanted to add another glamorous and highly themed resort hotel to the Magic Kingdom resort area. During the planning process for this new resort, Disney executives and Imagineers initially looked back to the original plans for the Venetian. However, the Venetian concept was once again shelved in favor of a proposed Mediterranean Resort.

The Mediterranean would have been beautifully themed as a Greek island. It would have been enormous, featuring more than seven hundred guest rooms spread across twelve buildings. The Mediterranean would have offered numerous dining options with a Greek flair, as well as an extensive marina to both transport guests to and from the Magic Kingdom and to provide numerous other entertainment options.

While references to a Mediterranean Resort were announced as being "on the drawing boards" in the 1981 Annual Report of Walt Disney Productions, the company announced that the resort would actually open "mid decade" ten years later, in its 1991 Annual Report.

As part of the site planning and preparation activities for the Mediterranean Resort, a number of test pilings were driven into the shoreline of the Seven Seas Lagoon between the Contemporary and the Ticket and Transportation Center to confirm that the land was sturdy enough to support the construction of a large hotel complex. Unfortunately, those test pilings repeatedly sank into the ground and disappeared. The ground was too swampy to support the project in the absence of an enormous expenditure of funds on foundational work, which still might not be enough to fix the problem. As such, Disney's plans for the Mediterranean also sank.

Today, the prime piece of real estate between the Contemporary and the Ticket and Transportation Center remains vacant. Being the eternal Disney optimist that I am, I continue to hope that Disney Imagineers will one day find a way to address the foundational issues in this location and move forward with the Venetian, the Mediterranean, or some other new Disney hotel concept. Until that time, guests can only look at this now heavily wooded area when travelling on the Magic Kingdom monorail route and wonder what could have been.

CHAPTER NINETEEN

# Cypress Point Lodge and Buffalo Junction

*Near Fort Wilderness Campground, Disney will build the 700-room Wilderness Lodge. It will be paired...with the 600-room Buffalo Junction, and both will have an Old West flavor.*

— "Disney Shows Off Big Plans for '90s: 4th Park, 7 Hotels, Many Rides," *Orlando Sentinel*, January 15, 1990

Fans of the Old West have plenty of things to enjoy in Walt Disney World. Foremost is the Frontierland section of the Magic Kingdom, where guests can experience a funny and romanticized look at the Old South and the Old West, complete with a runaway mine train, a full-size steam locomotive, and a saloon (the Diamond Horseshoe). But the rootin' tootin' fun doesn't stop in the Magic Kingdom. Cow pokes looking for a place to hang up their spurs for the night can find accommodations at the Fort Wilderness Resort and Campground, a camping area combining cabins and RV parking that opened on November 19, 1971. Guests who enjoy a rustic atmosphere with a more sophisticated flare can find more luxurious accommodations at Disney's Wilderness Lodge, a majestic resort reminiscent of the grand national park lodges from the turn of the century.

Notwithstanding the many Old West experiences and accommodations that guests can enjoy in and around Walt Disney World today, Disney executives contemplated adding two additional resorts that would have paid homage to the Old West. One of them, Cypress Point Lodge, would combine both hotel rooms and romantic beachfront cabins. A second, Buffalo Junction, would feature a replica of a Old West town.

# The Cypress Point Lodge

One of the lesser known proposed resorts for Disney World was the Cypress Point Lodge. Unlike the Asian, Venetian, and Persian resorts which would have all been in the highest category of Disney hotels in terms of theming and guest offerings (what Disney refers to today as a "deluxe" resort), the proposed Cypress Point Lodge was to be more of a "moderate" or "value" resort, providing an option for budget-conscious guests.

Cypress Point was to have been constructed during the early 1980s on the shores of Bay Lake near Fort Wilderness. It was announced as being "on the drawing boards" in the 1981 Annual Report of Walt Disney Productions.

The resort would have been heavily themed as a rustic hunting lodge paying tribute to the great outdoors and the U.S. national parks such as Yosemite and Yellowstone. Cypress Point would have offered a combination of five-hundred-and-fifty hotel rooms and fifty standalone cabins as accommodation options for guests.

An internal publication circulated by Disney to its cast members, known as *Walt Disney World Eyes and Ears*, provided this description of Cypress Point in 1982:

> Cypress Point Lodge will be a medium-sized hotel facility, located on the south shore of Bay Lake near our Fort Wilderness Campground Resort. Encompassing 550 rooms and 50 log cabins on the beach, Cypress Point Lodge will offer a romantic notion of a turn-of-the-century hunting lodge secluded in a deep forest.

The inclusion of fifty cabins sitting on the waterfront would certainly have been one of the most unique and romantic accommodations in all of Disney World. In addition, Cypress Point would have featured two restaurants and a pool and beach area. Guests would have travelled to the Magic Kingdom primarily via watercraft.

Disney was so sure that Cypress Point Lodge would be constructed that it actually moved forward with site preparation activities. Unfortunately, plans for Cypress Point ultimately fell victim to the same issue that halted plans for so many other unrealized concepts: a downturn in the United States economy. However, unlike most other proposed Walt Disney World concepts that never came to be, guests should be happy that plans for Cypress Point were shelved because these plans evolved into a much grander, much more richly themed resort: Disney's Wilderness Lodge, which opened on May 28, 1994. The Wilderness Lodge remains one of the most popular resorts in all of Walt Disney World.

## Buffalo Junction

Imagine a frontier town from the 1800s sitting on the edge of the American frontier. Imagine shops, restaurants, and entertainment all themed to the Old West. Imagine an exciting cowboy stunt show set within a massive arena. To top it all off, imagine a steam locomotive providing transportation for residents of this living and breathing Western town. If plans for Buffalo Junction (also referred to as Wilderness Junction and Fort Wilderness Junction) had come to pass, it would have included all of these above elements and more.

During Michael Eisner's famous Disney Decade, a period of unprecedented growth for the Disney company during the 1990s, numerous projects were proposed for the Disney World theme parks. Many of them never made it off the drawing board and into the parks, including Buffalo Junction.

While many Disney World resorts offer amazing theming and attention to detail, Buffalo Junction would have taken resort theming to another level. If it had been constructed, it would have been in contention for the most highly themed resort in all of Disney World. Not only would the actual hotel have had an Old West theme, but an authentic replica of a fully functional frontier town would have surrounded it!

Buffalo Junction was to be located between Fort Wilderness and Wilderness Lodge. The resort would have featured six hundred guest rooms. Among the many guest offerings at Buffalo Junction would have been a petting zoo and an interactive Wild West stunt show set within a large arena.

One of the more exciting aspects of the proposed Buffalo Junction project, especially for railroad fans, was that the long since closed Fort Wilderness Railroad would have been resurrected to provide transportation between Fort Wilderness, Wilderness Lodge, and Buffalo Junction, connecting Disney's triumvirate of Western-themed resorts.

The Fort Wilderness Railroad was a steam-powered railroad that plied through Fort Wilderness between 1973 and 1977. The Fort Wilderness Railroad locomotives were slightly smaller that those used for the Walt Disney World Railroad in the Magic Kingdom at a 4/5 scale with a narrower gauge track. The Fort Wilderness Railroad eventually closed due to a myriad of problems, including extensive maintenance costs, logistical issues, and a significant noise problem due to the train whistle blowing all hours of the night (which guests staying at Fort Wilderness understandably did not appreciate).

In its 1990 Annual Report, the Disney company announced that "Buffalo Junction Resort" was on an "agenda" of building projects for the company. In 1993, Disney went a step further by not only announcing plans for a "Wilderness Junction Resort," but even an opening year:

> Disney's Wilderness Junction Resort, a companion to Wilderness Lodge, will be a log-sided structure deep in the woods at the end of a nature trail. With 575 guest rooms, it will open in 1997.

Why did Disney not move forward with a project that included so many exciting elements? As was the case with the Cypress Point Lodge, a downturn in the United States economy led to plans for Buffalo Junction being cancelled. The recession of the late 1980s and early 1990s understandably made Disney hesitant about spending dollars on new projects, especially resorts.

A 1992 article in the *Orlando Sentinel* by Vicki Vaughan entitled "Disney Decade Revamped by Recession, Gulf War Plans for Another Park and Boardwalk Stalled, But Hotels Moved Forward" declared that Michael Eisner, in planning for the Disney Decade "hadn't counted on a Mideast war and lengthy recession that would ravage tourism," and further stated that "the recession, which sent Disney World's attendance plummeting an estimated 13 percent last year, has prompted subtle shifts in strategy." Specifically relating to Buffalo Junction, the article stated, "[a]ll-suite luxury hotels—the Mediterranean and Buffalo Junction—also have been put on hold." As it turned out, plans for Buffalo Junction were eventually moved from "on hold" to cancelled altogether.

## Finding Old West Fun in Walt Disney World Today

Of course, all is not lost for Disney World fans who love classic Westerns or the Old West. Far from it. Frontierland always has been, and always will be, an integral part of the Magic Kingdom, offering rip-roaring fun for cowboys and cowgirls of all ages.

While Cypress Point Lodge was never constructed, the majestic Wilderness Lodge replaced it. From the moment guests step into the grand lobby of Wilderness Lodge, complete with two fifty-five foot tall totem poles and an amazing eighty-two foot tall stone fireplace, they are transported to a grand national park lodge set in the great Pacific Northwest. Even if it is one hundred degrees in the central Florida heat, the crackling fireplace in the Wilderness Lodge lobby seems right at home.

Fort Wilderness continues to offer both cabins and RV parking areas for Disney World guests who want to stay in a more rustic setting. At Fort Wilderness, guests can partake in activities such as horseback riding, archery, and fishing, as well as a popular rip-roaring dinner show known as the Hoop-Dee-Doo Musical Revue. While the Fort Wilderness Railroad was never resurrected, remnants of its track can still be found in certain areas of the Fort Wilderness grounds.

For those longing for romantic cabins on the beach like the ones originally planned for Cypress Point Lodge, Disney made the exciting announcement in 2016 that the Copper Creek Villas and Cabins would be added to the Wilderness Lodge grounds. As an expansion of that resort's existing Disney Vacation Club complex, these cabins will sit on the shores of Bay Lake and serve as a fond reminder of the original plans for Cypress Point Lodge.

CHAPTER TWENTY

# Pop Century: The Legendary Years

*Experience the unforgettable fads of the 1950s through the 1990s all over again. From yo-yos and Play-Doh to Rubik's Cube and roller-blades, this resort hotel salutes the timeless fashions, catch phrases, toys and dances that captivated the world through the decades.*

— The Walt Disney Company (in reference to Disney's Pop Century Resort)

In recent years, "urban exploration" has grown into somewhat of a cultural phenomenon. Urban exploration (which is also referred to by a variety of other terms including draining, urban spelunking, and building hacking) involves the exploration of buildings, streets, amusement parks, drains, tunnels, and a variety of other man-made structures that have been abandoned and lay in varying degrees of disrepair or ruin. In many cases, these areas have been completely reclaimed by nature. A variety of blogs and online social groups have added to the popularity of urban exploration, including the widespread attention garnered by many stunning and dramatic photographs of these surreal, ominous, gloomy, and fascinating areas.

Examples of these abandoned structures and man-made elements can be found in a variety of locations, including decaying areas of major metropolitan cities, nuclear test sites, completely abandoned islands, and, believe it or not, at Walt Disney World. I'm not talking about the Haunted Mansion in the Magic Kingdom or the Twilight Zone Tower of Terror in Hollywood Studios, which are "themed" as abandoned structures. Instead, I'm referring to a proposed Disney World resort that was suddenly halted midway through its construction in 2001. It then sat frozen in time for more than ten years as surrounding vegetation slowly crept into its foundations and structural elements, creating an eerie Disney World ghost town. Even stranger, these very un-Disney structures actually remained in view of some guests. It's a story that can only be described as "legendary."

## The Pop Century Resort

Disney's Pop Century Resort opened on December 14, 2003. Pop Century was the fourth "value resort" constructed by Disney, following the All-Star Movies, All-Star Music, and All-Star Sports resorts. A value resort is a Disney designation for hotels that offer accommodations at the lowest price point on Disney property. Value resorts are good options for guests who want to stay inside the Disney bubble while not spending the large amounts of money required to stay at a deluxe resort such as the Contemporary or the Polynesian Village.

Pop Century celebrates the pop culture icons and elements of the 1950s, 1960s, 1970s, 1980s, and 1990s. The original plans for Pop Century called for two separate resort areas. Pop Century: The Classic Years was the designation for the portion of Pop Century that did open to guests. In addition, Pop Century would have also included the Legendary Years, which would have celebrated pop cultural elements from the 1900s, 1910s, 1920s, 1930s, and 1940s. The Classic Years and Legendary Years sections of Pop Century would have been separated by Hourglass Lake, a large body of water unsurprisingly shaped as an hourglass, and connected by Generation Gap Bridge. Construction for both halves of Pop Century began in 1999.

## The September 11 Attacks

The coordinated series of terror attacks on September 11, 2001, in New York City and Arlington, Virginia, as well as the attempted attack on Washington D.C., changed the United States forever. One of those impacts was economic, as the U.S. stock market closed for four consecutive trading days, an event unprecedented since the Great Depression. When the markets finally reopened, the Dow suffered its worse one-day drop in history. This had a trickle-down effect on a recession that had already begun earlier in 2001. Not surprisingly, the travel industry in the United States suffered dramatically. As a result, the Disney company halted construction on the entire Pop Century Resort. David Koening described the significant effect of the September 11 attacks on the Disney company in his book *Realityland: True-Life Adventures at Walt Disney World* (2007):

> At some hotels, entire floors were closed off to guests. Construction on the first phase of the 5,760-room Pop Century budget resort, which had already been slowed by recession, was halted.

When the economy eventually started to improve, work resumed on Pop Century: The Classic Years. It opened in December of 2003 with a total of two-thousand-eight-hundred-and-eighty guest rooms. The resort celebrates the "pop culture" of the 1950s through the 1990s, with bold colors and over-sized representations of popular items from those decades: bowling pins and a juke box (1950s); a yo-yo, Play-Doh, and a peace sign (1960s); an 8-track tape and disco dancing (1970s); a Rubik's Cube, a Walkman, and my personal favorite, a statue of Roger Rabbit (1980s); and a cell phone and a laptop (1990s).

Although the United States economy was improving, the demand still did not exist to justify moving forward with the second half of the project. As such, the Legendary Years section of Pop Century remained uncompleted.

A series of Legendary Years buildings sat in a ghostly, partially constructed state, including what would have been the central registration building for the resort, Legendary Hall. In surprisingly non-Disney fashion, these "structural skeletons" were within view of some guest rooms at Pop Century.

In the coming years, vegetation encroached into the concrete foundations of the Legendary Years buildings and vandals and the elements broke windows and decayed roofs. Disney primarily used the area for storage, but little care was given to the buildings themselves, and the entire site fell into a state of disrepair. The Legendary Years section of the Pop Century Resort more closely resembled a ghost town than any pop culture tribute to the first half of the century. Because of this, some guests began referring to the hotel complex as the Pop "Half" Century, given that only the 1950s through the 1990s were actually represented.

## Disney's Art of Animation

After ten years of sitting in a spooky, half-finished state, the Disney company finally moved forward with completing a resort on that site. However, instead of a Legendary Years continuation of Pop Century, Disney instead constructed what would become known as the Art of Animation Resort.

Art of Animation is divided into four distinct sections with themes based on four classic films: *The Little Mermaid* (1989), *The Lion King* (1994), *Finding Nemo* (2003), and *Cars* (2006). The resort opened in May 2012 in the value category offering approximately nine hundred guest rooms and, notably, more than one thousand family suites, a first for Disney's value resorts.

## Abandoned Elements in Disney Today

For urban explorers looking for abandoned areas in Walt Disney World to investigate, the options are now much more limited (and extremely frowned upon by the Disney company). Discovery Island, a roughly eleven-and-a-half acre island located in the middle of Bay Lake, was open to guests from 1974 through 1999 as a wildlife observation area. Since its closing, wildlife and dense vegetation are rumored to have completely overtaken Discovery Island.

Another "abandoned" Disney World area is River Country, a water park themed as an "old swimming hole" that opened in 1976 on the shores of Bay Lake. River County closed to the public in 2001, and since that time the park's pools and water slides have fallen into a state of disrepair with the surrounding vegetation slowly reclaiming the area. Portions of River County can be seen via boat transportation on Bay Lake, and in recent years pictures of the abandoned grounds have circulated widely on the internet.

The Walt Disney Company makes clear that visitors/trespassers on both Discovery Island and River Country grounds are strictly prohibited.

# Conclusion

*There's really no secret to our approach. We keep moving forward, opening up new doors and doing new things, because we're curious...and curiosity keeps leading us down new paths. We're always exploring and experimenting.*

— Walt Disney

I love Walt Disney World. There is no doubt about that. Why else would I spend countless hours working on this book? This love arises for a number of different reasons, but primarily because Disney World makes me feel like a kid again.

As a child growing up in the small, rural Alabama town of Speake, I used my imagination to turn cow pastures and barns into a world of pirates and astronauts, Davy Crockett and Apple Dumpling gangs, Ichabod and Mr. Toad. Yes, I lived in the wonderful world of Disney, where anything was possible and the only limitations were those imposed by my imagination (which, for me, was no limitation at all).

Sure, eventually I grew up (sorry, Peter Pan), but I suppose I will always be a kid at heart. When I am fortunate enough to visit Disney World, I completely return to that state of mind. All the stresses and worries that I may have at that particular time melt away. I become the kid that I once was, ready to explore distant jungles, ride in pirate ships, fly in rockets, visit different worlds, and experience adventure in all shapes and sizes.

Perhaps it is that "child at heart" naïve amazement that gets to me when I think about the brilliant concepts that never came to be in Walt Disney World. The unbridled imagination that I once used as a child to entertain myself on otherwise boring days gets dusted off and begins churning once more. While the details we know about these proposed concepts from artistic renderings, corporate disclosures, promotional materials, and other resources guide that daydreaming exercise, the imagination I once used as a child fills in all of the creative gaps.

I hope this book has rekindled, at least to some extent, that same childhood imagination and wonder in each of you. Whether you are strolling around World Showcase or the Magic Kingdom on your next trip, or are thinking about the Most Magical Place on Earth during a "mental break" at work, I hope you daydream of the magnificence of Thunder Mesa in Frontierland, the culture and scope of a Soviet Union Pavilion in World Showcase, the wackiness of Roger Rabbit's Toontown in Disney's Hollywood Studios, and the unique adventure that would have been Beastly Kingdom in Disney's Animal Kingdom.

For my part, the most exciting concept that never came to be is the one that I don't even know about. It is the breathtaking plan that never saw the light of day. As I mentioned in the Introduction, the Disney company's most creative minds have spent decades developing amazing lands, attractions, and experiences for Disney World, many of which never made it off the drawing board. Could there be an attraction concept that we don't know about that was grander than Thunder Mesa? More beautiful than the Enchanted Snow Palace? More innovative than Fire Mountain? More nostalgic than Mickey's Movieland? Could there be such an idea locked behind closed doors in the offices of Walt Disney Imagineering?

Of course there is...just sitting high atop a creative shelf gathering dust and waiting to be re-discovered....

# Acknowledgments

Although I have enjoyed reading books since I was a child, the thought of actually writing my own book never crossed my mind until a couple of years ago. After having spent more time than I care to admit trying to complete this project, I have a whole new respect for writers. The process of putting pen to paper and fingers to keyboard in an effort to create something that you are proud of and that others will enjoy is far more difficult than I could have ever imagined. To the extent that I have accomplished those goals, the real credit should go to the people listed below.

First and foremost, I want to send a heartfelt thank you to my wife, Alexis. As is the case with every other aspect of my life, Alexis was overwhelmingly supportive and encouraging of my work on this book. My professional work schedule is time intensive, as is my "father schedule." There are not many spare hours available to write a book. Instead, a great deal of family time, vacation time, and otherwise quality time with Alexis had to be sacrificed to complete this book. I'm sure at many points she was frustrated at the sight of me poring through annual shareholder reports for the Disney company while she was forced to take on a larger portion of the household duties. However, Alexis never complained and instead continued to support and encourage me, even when my own enthusiasm for the project started to wane. To use a football analogy, there is no doubt that I "outkicked my coverage." Thank you for being my best friend and, even more importantly, The One.

To my mother, Gradie Mae Smith, thank you for being the kindest and strongest woman that I have ever known. The example you continue to set inspires me on a daily basis. I have always known that, notwithstanding any mistakes I may have made in my life, I could still find unconditional love and understanding from you. In writing this book, I knew that no matter how terrible it might be for a "neutral" reader, you would swear it was the greatest book ever written.

To my father, Edmon Smith, I don't even know how to put a thank you into words. But thank you for being the best man I have ever known. You have worked countless hours to support our family, and I could never repay you for that. All I have ever wanted to be is you, but I realize that is an unrealistic goal. However, if I can even become half the man, husband, and father that you are, I will have achieved a tremendous goal indeed.

To my oldest son Dakota, thank you for being such a kind and genuine young man, for inspiring me to be a better man each and every day, and for being a great role model to your siblings. You have insisted on carving your own path in life, and I could not be prouder of that. Fortunately, I passed along all of my good characteristics to you (as few as they are) and none of my bad ones. Our trips to Walt Disney World when you were a child are some of my favorite memories, and played a key roll in inspiring this book. Keep being your own man and stay true to yourself...and also feel free to spend a boring afternoon with your dad every now and then.

To my beautiful twins, Samuel and Scarlett, and my youngest daughter, Alice Anne, thank you for showing me what true joy and happiness really are. Even when I have had a discouraging day, the sight of your smiles when I walk in the door each night continually reminds me of what is important in life. As I write this, Alexis and I are planning Samuel and Scarlett's first trip to Disney World. I hope that all three of you can find some of the joy in this magical place that I continue to have, and I hope you see that joy in the pages of this book when you are old enough to read it.

I want to also send out a big thanks to my editor, Bob McLain, without whom this book would not have been possible. Bob and I had never met or talked until the day that I sent him a book idea about the Walt Disney World that never was. Bob is a fantastic editor, and has been a part of some of the most entertaining books about Disney ever written, many of which graced my bookshelves long before I ever considered writing my own book. Much to my surprise, Bob did respond to my original idea, which created a dialogue that eventually resulted in this book. I'm sure Bob had to do much more work on this project than he normally does. [*That's not true. Bob*] But thank you Bob for giving me a chance, for being extremely patient as a corporate attorney "tried" to write a book, and for turning whatever the heck it was I sent to you into this finished product.

I also want to thank my good friend David Block who, as it turns out, is a pretty darn good editor in his own right. David contributed many great ideas and thoughts about the structure and content of this book. He was also brave enough to actually read over these chapters and provide invaluable input and suggested revisions. Hopefully this acknowledgement is enough to make up for whatever hours he had to sacrifice from his other duties as a devoted football manager. Not Pop Warner...fantasy.

As strange as it may sound, I must also thank both Walt and Roy Disney for creating my favorite place on Earth, Walt Disney World. During the dedication ceremony for the Magic Kingdom, Roy stated: "May Walt Disney World bring joy and inspiration and new knowledge to all who come to this happy place...a Magic Kingdom where the young at heart of all ages can laugh and play and learn together." If Roy and Walt were alive today,

I would tell them that Disney World has certainly brought me joy, inspiration, new knowledge, and so much more. I always tell people that Disney World is truly a magical place. It is more than just bricks and mortar, rides and shows, hamburgers and hot dogs. It is a place where adults can become kids again and a place where dreams really can come true.

Finally, I thank you, the reader. A dream of writing a book really doesn't mean much if nobody is there to read it. By taking the time to acquire and read this book, you have made a lifelong dream come true, and I am eternally grateful for that.

# About the Author

Christopher E. Smith is a lucky husband, a proud father, and a blessed son. He is also a corporate attorney practicing law in Huntsville, Alabama. Chris lives in Huntsville with his wife, Alexis; his sons, Dakota and Samuel; and his daughters, Scarlett and Alice Anne.

Chris graduated from the University of Alabama in 2001 with a Bachelor of Arts degree in History and Political Science. He graduated summa cum laude from the University of Alabama School of Law in 2004 where he was awarded the M. Leigh Harrison Award, the law school's highest academic honor.

He first visited Walt Disney World in 1984 at the age of 7. That inaugural trip to the Most Magical Place on Earth forever shaped his outlook on life. As a child growing up in rural Speake, Alabama, Chris was accustomed to seeing cow pastures, barns, and cornfields. He certainly did not know what to make of the "magic" of Cinderella Castle, Space Mountain, Pirates of the Caribbean, or 20,000 Leagues Under the Sea. But that Disney magic did put a smile on his face that has been there ever since. He was hooked on Disney World from the very beginning.

Chris has visited Disney World dozens of times with his family and friends over the course of the roughly thirty-three years since that initial trip. During that time, he has realized what so many other Disney fans already know, that Disney World truly is a magical place.

When he is not spending time with his family, practicing law, or studying the history of Walt Disney World, Chris is cheering on his beloved alma mater, the University of Alabama. Roll Tide!

# More Books from Theme Park Press

## History Made Magical

The history BEHIND the history of some of Walt Disney World's iconic Magic Kingdom locations and attractions, including the Jungle Cruise, Crystal Palace, and Main Street, U.S.A. Learn where the Imagineers got THEIR ideas.

**themeparkpress.com/books/historical-tour-disney-world.htm**

## The Rosetta Stone of Disney Magic

Warning! There be secrets ahead. Disney secrets. Mickey doesn't want you to know how the magic is made, but Jim Korkis knows, and if you read Jim's book, you'll know, too. Put the kids to bed. Pull those curtains. Power down that iPhone. Let's keep this just between us...

**themeparkpress.com/books/secret-stories-disney-world.htm**

## A Year in the Life of Disneyland

And what a year! In 1955, Walt Disney's dream of a theme park, the first of its kind in the world, came true. Disney historian Jim Korkis' entertaining tale of an American pop culture icon is power-packed with details, and the most thorough account of Disneyland's early days ever published.

themeparkpress.com/books/disneyland-1955.htm

## Disney the World Over

Clemson University professor Stephanie Barczewski delivers a scholarly but accessible comparative history of the Disney theme parks, from Anaheim to Shanghai, with a focus on the engineering, cultural, and political challenges that Disney overcame to build its "happiest places" across the globe.

themeparkpress.com/books/magic-kingdoms.htm

**Four Decades with Disney**

Disney Legend William "Sully" Sullivan got his start in 1955 with Walt Disney and Disneyland, taking tickets for the Jungle Cruise. Forty years later he retired as vice-president of Magic Kingdom. This is his never-before-told story.

**themeparkpress.com/books/sullivan-jungle-cruise-legend.htm**

**The Story of Walt's EPCOT**

Disney historian and urban planner Sam Gennawey traces the evolution of the EPCOT we didn't get and the Epcot we did, in a tour-de-force analysis of Walt's vision for city-building and how his City of Tomorrow might have turned out had he lived.

**themeparkpress.com/books/progress-city.htm**

Printed in Great Britain
by Amazon

81216139R00108